Giggle Giggle Snort Tee Hee Ho Ho Guffaw Guffaw

CATCH OF THE DAY

And what a catch you are!
We hope Sherman and his
crew will bring a smile or two.
Get well soon, Ticker. You are
constantly in our thoughts, our prayers.
Much love,

Becky
+ Pat

Giggle Chuckle Chuckle Silly Silly Ha Ha Tee Hee Funny Funny Woo-hoo Har dee har har

Smile

Other Books by Jim Toomey

Sherman's Lagoon: Ate That, What's Next?

Poodle: The Other White Meat

An Illustrated Guide to Shark Etiquette

Another Day in Paradise

Greetings from Sherman's Lagoon

Surf's Up!

The Shark Diaries

Treasury

Sherman's Lagoon 1991 to 2001: Greatest Hits and Near Misses

CATCH OF THE DAY

The Eighth Sherman's Lagoon Collection

by Jim Toomey

TODAY'S SPECIAL
CARTOON SHARK ALL-U-CAN-STAND

Andrews McMeel Publishing

Kansas City

Sherman's Lagoon is distributed internationally by King Features Syndicate, Inc. For information, write King Features Syndicate, Inc., 888 Seventh Avenue, New York, New York 10019.

 For information, write Andrews McMeel Publishing, an Andrews McMeel Universal company, 4520 Main Street, Kansas City, Missouri 64111.

05 06 07 08 BBG 10 9 8 7 6 5 4 3

ISBN-13: 978-0-7407-4670-3

ISBN-10: 0-7407-4670-7

Library of Congress Control Number: 2004103571

Sherman's Lagoon may be viewed on the Internet at
www.shermanslagoon.com.

To Robin

MEGAN, I THINK I'M GOING TO PUT TOGETHER A RETRO 60'S ROCK BAND.

WE COULD WRITE NEW SONGS THAT SOUND LIKE THOSE GREAT OLD TUNES FROM OUR YOUTH.

AND WE COULD REHEARSE MILES AND MILES FROM HERE.
YOU HAVE MY BLESSING.

FILLMORE, I'M PUTTING A BAND TOGETHER. I NEED YOU ON "HATCHET."
HUH?

"HATCHET" ... IT'S WHAT ROCKERS CALL A GUITAR.

AXE.
THAT'S WHAT I'M DOING. AXING YOU TO JOIN MY BAND.

SO, ARE YOU IN ON HATCHET OR NOT?
IF IT'LL END THIS DISCUSSION.

ERNEST, HOW WOULD YOU LIKE TO JOIN MY ROCK BAND?

I DON'T PLAY AN INSTRUMENT.
THAT'S OKAY. WE JUST NEED YOU TO DRAW IN THE YOUNGER AUDIENCE.

YOU JUST HAVE TO STAND THERE AND LOOK CUTE... MAYBE SHAKE A TAMBOURINE.

SO, I'M YOUR DANNY PARTRIDGE?
TRACY, ACTUALLY. DANNY STOOD THERE AND HELD A BASS.

HAWTHORNE, WOULD YOU MANAGE MY NEW RETRO BAND... "SHERMAN'S HERMITS"?
HMPH.

DO YOU HAVE ANY TALENT?
NOPE.
WELL, DO YOU HAVE THE DRIVE TO PUT IN THE LONG HOURS IT WILL TAKE?
NOT REALLY.

DO YOU HAVE A PROBLEM WITH ME RIPPING YOU OFF BLINDLY?
I'D EXPECT IT.

OKAY! SHERMAN'S HERMITS FIRST BAND REHEARSAL. LET'S GROOVE, BROTHERS.

TEST! TEST! ONE, TWO! ONE, TWO!

CHECK! TEST! CHECK, CHECK, ONE, TWO!

ALL RIGHT! LET'S JUST HEAR YOUR SONG!
THAT WAS THE SONG.

OKAY, GUYS, LET'S HAVE A GOOD REHEARSAL TODAY.

I'VE WRITTEN A NEW SONG, WITH A BEATLES FEEL TO IT.
COOL.

AND, IN THE SPIRIT OF THE 60'S, IT'S WRITTEN ABOUT MY ONE TRUE LOVE.
MEGAN?

DONUTS.
"EIGHT GLAZED A WEEK"?

Sherman's Lagoon

WHAT'CHA DOIN', ERNEST?
I TOOK ONE OF THE SONGS OUR BAND RECORDED AND PUT IT IN MY MACINTOSH.

THEN I ADDED ACCORDIAN, UPPED THE TEMPO, AND THREW IN A LITTLE RIFF ON THE BASS.

I GOTTA ADMIT, IT'S REALLY MADE IT, UH...

TOP 40 MATERIAL?
... NOT AS LAME.

HOLD IT! STOP WHATEVER BAD SONG YOU'RE WORKING ON!

ERNEST REMIXED YOUR FIRST SONG WITH HIS COMPUTER AND NOW IT'S A SMASH HIT ON THE POLKA TOP 40!

WE FINALLY NAILED THAT DEMOGRAPHIC WE WERE AFTER!

MILLIONS OF BABY BOOMERS LONGING FOR THE 60'S?
3 GUYS IN FARGO.

HAWTHORNE, THESE OUTFITS ARE AWFUL.
LOOK, YOU GUYS ARE A POLKA BAND NOW.

AND POLKA FANS EXPECT CERTAIN THINGS FROM THEIR BANDS. THE LEDERHOSEN AND THE HATS ARE PART OF IT.

WHAT ELSE?
YOUR BREATH NEEDS WORK.

MY BREATH?
YEAH. IT'S NOT SAUSAGEY ENOUGH.

THE BIG SHOW'S ABOUT TO START. YOU GUYS READY TO PLAY?
HAWTHORNE, HOW ARE WE GOING TO DO THIS CONCERT?
BACK STAGE

OUR SONGS ARE DONE BY A COMPUTER IN A SOUND STUDIO. WE DON'T ACTUALLY PLAY THEM.
LIP SYNCH! NO ONE WILL KNOW!
BACK STAGE

TECHNICALLY, NONE OF US HAS LIPS.
YEAH
GET OUT THERE!!

HOW'S THE NEW SONG COMING ALONG, BOYS?
OKAY.

WHAT'S IT CALLED?
POLKA, POLKA, POLKA.

BUT IT NEEDS SOMETHING.

ANOTHER "POLKA."
BRILLIANT.

HOLD IT! HOLD IT!

WHAT? I THOUGHT THE SONG WAS GOING GREAT.

THAT'S THE PROBLEM. IT'S GOING TOO WELL. TOO CIVILIZED.
HUH?

VH1 IS COMING HERE TO FILM A "BEHIND THE MUSIC" SEGMENT ON US, AND IT'LL BE THE MOST BORING ONE EVER.

ERNEST, THROW A PUNCH AT FILLMORE.
IF IT'LL HELP THE BAND.

BAD NEWS, GUYS... WE'LL HAVE TO BREAK UP THE BAND.
HUH?

YEP. BIG ARTICLE IN THE POLKA POPULAR PRESS REVEALING THAT YOU'RE PHONIES.
"POLKA DOTS" PHONIES

THIS IS THE ROLLING STONE OF THE POLKA INDUSTRY, SO YOU GUYS ARE TOAST.

BOTH READERS SAW IT.
THE OOMPAH'S DEAD.

AHH, HERE COMES LUNCH NOW.
DON'T YOU EVER FEEL CRUEL?

HEY, I'M JUST A CARNIVORE DOING WHAT COMES NATURAL.

NOW, JERRY, ON THE OTHER HAND... WHAT HE DOES IS CRUEL.

HE TICKLES 'EM FIRST.
STOP IT!
HEE HEE
HEH HEH
OOOM HOO HOO

SHERMAN, DO YOU THINK THE SPARK IS GONE FROM OUR MARRIAGE?
HECK, NO.

THEN SAY SOMETHING SPONTANEOUSLY ROMANTIC TO ME.
ALL RIGHT.

NACHOS.
I'LL TAKE IT.

SHERMAN'S LAGOON

SHERMAN, WE HAVE A STRESS DISTRIBUTION PROBLEM. I HAVE TOO MUCH OF IT, AND YOU... YOU DON'T SEEM TO HAVE ANY.

YOU HAVE THE UNCANNY ABILITY TO RELAX ANYWHERE.
INNER PEACE IS NOT EASY TO ATTAIN, MEGAN. IT TAKES...

Z Z Z Z Z Z

I WAS REFERRING YOUR ABILITY TO FALL ASLEEP IN MID-SENTENCE.
HUH?

LOOK, SHERMAN. THE ANSWER TO OUR PROBLEMS.
THE ZEN CENTER?

"FIND PEACE THROUGH MEDITATION... SESSIONS ARE THREE TIMES A DAY FOR A WEEK."

ARE YOU SURE IT'S WORTH ALL THE EFFORT?

I'M GONNA FIND PEACE IF IT KILLS ME!
EASY, GANDHI.

HEY, MEGAN, WHAT ARE YOU DOING?
SHHH. I'M TRYING TO FIND PEACE THROUGH MEDITATION.
DORITOS

I NEED ABSOLUTE QUIET TO FIND NIRVANA.
DORITOS

DORITOS

CRUNCH ONE DORITO AND YOU'RE A DEAD FISH.
GULP.
DORITOS

HI. MEGAN AND SHERMAN CHECKING IN.
ALRIGHTEE. JUST A MOMENT.
ZEN CENTER

I DON'T HAVE ALL DAY. I'VE GOT PEACE TO FIND!
ZEN CENTER

WE DON'T RAISE OUR VOICES HERE AT THE ZEN CENTER.
ZEN CENTER

THEN HOW DO YOU YELL?
CODE LAVENDER. CODE LAVENDER.
ZEN CENTER

MY NAME IS SKYE. I'LL BE YOUR MEDITATION INSTRUCTOR.

EVERYONE CLOSE HIS OR HER EYES AND START THINKING PEACEFUL THOUGHTS.

EXCUSE ME, SKYE... CAN I SMACK THE NOSE WHISTLER HERE?

IN ORDER TO ACHIEVE THE PROPER STATE OF MIND FOR MEDITATION, YOU MUST GO TO A HAPPY PLACE IN YOUR HEAD.

A PEACEFUL MEADOW, A STILL MOUNTAIN LAKE...

ANY PLACE THAT BRINGS YOU JOY.

MINE'S A BIG SALE AT Q.V.C.
SIZZLER COMMERCIAL.

REMEMBER, CLASS, FIND A MANTRA YOU CAN KEEP YOUR WHOLE LIFE.

OHMMM... OHMMMM...
GOOD.

AHHH CHI, AHHHH CHI...
EXCELLENT. VERY CALMING.

ROHHHHHXANNE!
NEEDS WORK.

YOU WANTED TO SEE US, SKYE?
MEGAN, SHERMAN, WE'RE GOING TO NEED YOU TO LEAVE.

YOUR PERSONALITIES JUST DON'T FIT HERE AT THE ZEN CENTER.

WE FEEL YOU'D BE BETTER OFF FINDING PEACE AT, SAY, UH... OH...

A SPA?
A TRACTOR PULL.

HOW WAS THE ZEN CENTER, SHERMAN?
I LEARNED A LOT ABOUT MYSELF.

SUCH AS?
I CAN FIND JOY AND FULLFILLMENT USING JUST MY BRAIN.

AND A GEORGE FOREMAN GRILL.
DEEP.

SHERMAN'S LAGOON

HEY, "UNDERWATER FEAR FACTOR" IS GOING TO DO A SHOW HERE AT THE LAGOON.
Lagoon Tribune
GROUPER RUNS FOR

TRYOUTS ARE TOMORROW. MAYBE I'LL GO.
Lagoon Tribune
GROUPER RUNS FOR

Lagoon Tribune
GROUPER

DON'T YOU HAVE A FEAR OF TRYOUTS?
OH, RIGHT.
GROUPER RUNS FOR

NAME?
SHERMAN.
BIGGEST FEAR?
FEAR FACTOR TRYOUTS

NO, WAIT... LET ME GUESS. A SHARK'S BIGGEST FEAR WOULD BE HAVING TO ACTUALLY EAT A SALAD.
FEAR FACTOR TRYOUTS

FEAR FACTOR TRYOUTS

YEAH, OKAY. GO WITH THAT.
NEXT.
FEAR FACTOR TRYOUTS

NAME?
FILLMORE.
BIGGEST FEAR?
FEAR FACTOR TRYOUTS

OH, YOU NAME IT. BUGS, HEIGHTS, SPEED, MOST FOODS, PAIN... DID I MENTION BUGS?
FEAR FACTOR TRYOUTS

SIGN RIGHT HERE.
FEAR FACTOR TRYOUTS

I'M AFRAID OF USED PENS.
I'LL JUST WRITE "VERBAL AGREEMENT."
FEAR FACTOR TRYOUTS

NAME?
HAWTHORNE.
BIGGEST FEAR?
FEAR FACTOR TRYOUTS

NOTHING.
OH, COME ON.
FEAR FACTOR TRYOUTS

BUGS? HEIGHTS? BEING STUCK NUDE IN PUBLIC?
FEAR FACTOR TRYOUTS

SCRATCH THAT LAST ONE.
ARE WE FILMING YET?
FEAR FACTOR TRYOUTS

WELL, LOOKS LIKE WE ALL QUALIFIED TO BE CONTESTANTS ON "FEAR FACTOR."

BUT, WE ALL KNOW HOW IT'S GOING TO TURN OUT. IT'S A WELL KNOWN FACT THAT GREAT WHITE SHARKS HAVE NO NATURAL PREDATORS, AND THEREFORE, HAVE NO SENSE OF FEAR.

BZZZZZZZZZZZ

SPLASH!
AUGH!

OKAY, CONTESTANTS, FOR THE FIRST ROUND OF "FEAR FACTOR" YOU HAVE TO SIT IN A VAT OF SEA SLUGS. SHERMAN, YOU FIRST.

I ROUTINELY BATHE IN SEA SLUGS. IT'S GOOD FOR THE COMPLEXION.
YOU'RE ON TV. AT LEAST ACT LIKE YOU'RE GROSSED OUT.

OH, GROSS, GROSS! I'M SITTING IN A VAT OF SEA SLUGS. I DON'T KNOW HOW MUCH LONGER I CAN STAND IT!

COULD I GET A HOT TOWEL AND A MINERAL WATER?
CUT.

FOR OUR NEXT ROUND OF "FEAR FACTOR," EACH OF YOU MUST GO INSIDE THIS WHALE AND RING THE BELL IN THE BACK OF HIS STOMACH. WHOEVER DOES IT QUICKEST WINS.

HAWTHORNE, YOU'RE UP FIRST. GO!
GURGLE GURGLE BLURP!

TICK TICK TICK TICK
BLURP! GURGLE! WHOOSH! WHOOSH!

CLOCK'S TICKING.
I'M WAITING FOR THE RINSE CYCLE TO END.
TICK TICK TICK TICK
WHOOSH! WHOOSH!

THIS NEXT "FEAR FACTOR" CHALLENGE INVOLVES A BOTTOM DWELLER.
URP!

OUR CONTESTANTS WILL BE PLACED IN AN AIRTIGHT VAULT WITH HIM.

LAST ONE REMAINING WINS.
WHAT'S SO HARD ABOUT THAT?

HE'S BEEN ON AN INTERVENOUS CHILI DRIP FOR 8 HOURS.
AAUUUGH!
URP!

THIS IS IT! THE FINAL ROUND. WHOEVER EATS THE MOST JELLY FISH WILL BE OUR "FEAR FACTOR" CHAMPION.

AUGH! GROSS!

WE SEA TURTLES LOVE A GOOD JELLY FISH.

MY SISTER AND I USED TO FIGHT OVER THE RED ONES.
GROSS!
GAME OVER.

Sherman's Lagoon

I CAN'T BELIEVE YOU WON ON "FEAR FACTOR."
YEP.

SO, WHAT ARE YOU GONNA DO WITH THE PRIZE MONEY?

OH, YOU KNOW ME... I GAVE IT TO CHARITY.

HI, CHARITY.
WE'RE STILL NOT DATING.

I BET I COULD BE A TALK SHOW HOST.
IT'S NOT SO EASY.

YOU'D REALLY HAVE TO DEVOTE YOURSELF TO SOMETHING LIKE THAT... PUT YOUR HEART INTO IT... GIVE IT 110%.

I COULD DO IT WILLY NILLY.
IF ANYONE COULD...

SO, YOU'LL BE THE PRODUCER OF MY TALK SHOW?
YOU BET.

I'LL FOLLOW YOUR LEAD. YOU CALL THE SHOTS. **YOU** ARE THE BOSS AROUND HERE.

WHY DON'T I HAVE A COFFEE?
I'LL GET THAT.

I'M STARTING MY OWN CABLE ACCESS TALK SHOW.
UH, OH.

AND IT'S GONNA BE COMPLETELY ORIGINAL. NOTHING LIKE IT. HAWTHORNE HERE IS MY WRITER/PRODUCER.

CHECK OUT MY TOP TEN LIST.
LETTERMAN ALREADY DOES A TOP TEN LIST.

HE DOES?
HERE. MAKE IT A TOP NINE LIST.

THE FIRST GUEST ON MY TALK SHOW IS MY GOOD FRIEND FILLMORE THE SEA TURTLE. LET'S GIVE FILLMORE A BIG HAND.

THERE'S NOBODY IN THE AUDIENCE.
THE SHOW'S TAPED. WE PUT THE AUDIENCE SOUNDS IN LATER.

OH.

AS A MATTER OF FACT, IF YOU MOVE YOUR LIPS A LITTLE, WE CAN PUT YOUR SOUNDS IN, TOO.
I'D LIKE TO READ A POEM.

WE'RE ALMOST BACK FROM THE COMMERCIAL. YOU TWO NEED TO PICK IT UP.

ASK ME ABOUT MY STAMP COLLECTION. I JUST ACQUIRED A RARE TONGA AIRMAIL.
WE'RE BACK.
ALLLLRIGHTEE.

SO, FILLMORE, TELL ME ABOUT YOUR... UH...

EMBARRASSINGLY LONG DROUGHT WITH THE LADIES.
I DO JUST FINE!

WHO'S MY NEXT GUEST?
JUST READ THE CARD. IT'S A SURPRISE.

AND, WE'RE LIVE.
MY NEXT GUEST ON THE SHOW IS... THE GIANT SQUID?!!

AAAUUGHH!

NOW THAT'S QUALITY TELEVISION.
VERY SPRINGER-ESQUE.
AUGH!

OUR RATINGS WERE GREAT WHEN YOU FOUGHT THE GIANT SQUID ON YOUR TALK SHOW.
YEAH?

I SAY WE GO TO A TOTAL "SPRINGER" FORMAT! STARTING WITH TODAY'S SHOW!

BUT, WE DON'T EVEN HAVE A GUEST SCHEDULED.
GOOD POINT. UHHH... FIGHT WITH YOURSELF.

THIS IS ODD TELEVISION.
NOT IF YOU KNOW HIM.
OOF!
TAKE THAT!
OW!

TODAY ON MY TALK SHOW, OUR TOPIC IS "WIVES WHO NAG TOO MUCH."

EVERYONE SAY HELLO TO MY VERY OWN WIFE, MEGAN...

BOOO!
BOO
HISSSSSSSSSSS
BOO!

... WHO REPRESENTS NON-NAGGING WIVES.
NICE TRY, MISTER.

I HAVE A SPECIAL GUEST ON MY TALK SHOW TODAY. LET'S GIVE FLIPPER A BIG HAND.

FLIPPER, YOU'RE KNOWN FOR YOUR POPULAR 60'S TV SERIES, BUT WHAT HAVE YOU DONE SINCE THEN?

UHHH... WELL, I STILL APPEAR IN FLIPPER RE-RUNS.
LET ME PUT IT ANOTHER WAY... YOU, PERSONALLY. WHAT'S KEPT YOU BUSY FOR THE LAST FORTY YEARS?

IS THIS SOME KIND OF AMBUSH?
LET'S GO TO A COMMERCIAL.

TODAY ON OUR SHOW WE HAVE "CHARLIE THE TUNA," THE FAMOUS SPOKESFISH FOR STARKIST.
YO.

YOU'RE ACTUALLY THE FOURTH "CHARLIE THE TUNA" TO WORK FOR THE COMPANY.
DAT'S RIGHT.

SO, WHAT HAPPENED TO THE OTHER THREE?
DEY GOT RETIREMENT PACKAGES.

A RETIREMENT PACKAGE? FOR A TUNA?
YOU CAN BE PACKAGED IN OIL, YOU CAN BE PACKAGED IN SPRING WATUH.

AND WE'RE BACK FROM OUR COMMERCIAL BREAK WITH OUR NEW GUEST, SAM... TELL US A LITTLE ABOUT YOURSELF, SAM.

CAN THESE THINGS EVEN TALK? WHY DID YOU BOOK HIM ON A TALK SHOW IF HE CAN'T EVEN TALK?

OH, GROSS! GET A CLOSE-UP!!
PTUI!
SPLAT

Sherman's Lagoon

BAD NEWS, CHAMP. THAT WAS THE NETWORK ON THE PHONE. YOUR TALK SHOW'S BEEN CANCELLED.
HUH? WHY?
PRODUCER

TOO RISKÉ, TOO VIOLENT. YOU'RE AHEAD OF YOUR TIME. WE'LL HAVE TO WAIT FOR THE T.V. STANDARDS TO GET A LITTLE LOWER. HANG IN THERE.

PRODUCER
RING RING

THEY WANT 20 MORE SHOWS.
IT'S ABOUT TIME!
PRODUCER

IS IT TIME FOR YOUR ANNUAL MIGRATION TO ASCENSION ISLAND?
YEP. THIS IS THE YEAR I FIND MY MATE.

I CHECKED MY CHART. THE STARS ARE WITH ME.

MY GEMINI MOON IS RISING IN VIRGO.

SPEAKING OF YOUR MOON, IS THIS A SPEEDO?
PUT THAT BACK!

FILLMORE, A WORD OF ADVICE BEFORE YOU HEAD OFF TO ASCENSION ISLAND.
GO AHEAD.

WOMEN LIKE A TAKE-CHARGE, CONFIDENT MAN. YOU'RE THE BOSS!
THEY DO?

TRUST ME. IT DOESN'T MATTER WHAT YOU SAY, AS LONG AS YOU SAY IT WITH COMPLETE CONFIDENCE.

SHERMAN, WHEN ARE YOU GOING TO FOLD THE LAUNDRY?
7:15!

WELL, THIS IS IT. I'M OFF TO ASCENSION ISLAND.

THIS IS THE YEAR FOR YOU, FILLMORE. YOU'RE GONNA FIND THAT SHE-TURTLE.

YOU LOOK HANDSOME AND CONFIDENT. NOTHING CAN STOP YOU. GO GET 'EM, TIGER!
CIAO.

IS THAT HIS BOXER UNDERWEAR HANGING OUT OF HIS SHELL?
IT CAN'T POSSIBLY MATTER.

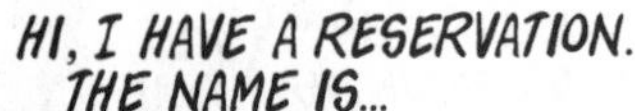

HI, I HAVE A RESERVATION. THE NAME IS...
MR. FILLMORE. YES. WELCOME TO ASCENSION ISLAND, SIR.
The Inn at Ascension Island
Registration

YOU'RE ALL SET... HERE'S YOUR KEY... SAME ROOM AS LAST YEAR... WE'RE DRAWING A HOT BATH FOR YOU RIGHT NOW.

WOW. THAT'S SERVICE. IT'S LIKE YOU KNEW I WAS ABOUT TO WALK THROUGH THE DOOR.
The Inn at Ascension Island
Registration

YOUR COLOGNE ARRIVED FIVE MINUTES AGO.
OH, GOOD. IT'S WORKING.
Registration

WHY, KIRSTIN. IT'S YOU. HI.
HELLO.

IMAGINE MY RUNNING INTO YOU AGAIN. IT MUST BE...

...YOU KNOW...

FATE.
STALKING?

HI, I'M FILLMORE.
I'M MONIQUE.

SO, COME HERE OFTEN?
EVERY MATING SEASON, LIKE ALL THE OTHER SEA TURTLES.

RIGHT.

SO, HOW AM I DOING SO FAR?
I LIKE YOU. YOU'RE PATHETIC.

HAWTHORNE, IT'S FILLMORE, HERE ON ASCENSION ISLAND. I MET A GREAT GIRL!

IT'S FILLMORE. SAYS HE MET SOMEONE.

SHE'S PERFECT. SHE EVEN LOVES MY COLOGNE.

WHAT'S SHE LIKE?
NOSELESS.

MONIQUE, I CAN'T WAIT TO TAKE YOU BACK HOME.
ME TOO, FILLMORE.

YOU'RE GONNA LOVE MY FRIENDS.
I'M SURE I WILL.

WE SIT AROUND FOR HOURS HAVING DEEP DISCUSSIONS ABOUT ALL KINDS OF THINGS.

LOOK! EITHER IT'S A BOOGER OR IT'S NOT!
WE'RE GONNA NEED A BIOPSY.

MONIQUE, I'VE NEVER HAD A SHE-TURTLE BE ATTRACTED TO ME. THEY USUALLY GO FOR THE MACHO TYPES.

NOT ME, FILLMORE. I LIKE THE SHY, QUIET TYPE. YOU KNOW WHAT THEY SAY... "THE MEEK SHALL INHERIT THE EARTH."
I HOPE SO.

SIGH.

BY THE WAY, DO YOU STAND TO INHERIT ANYTHING ELSE?
WHY DO YOU ASK?

FILLMORE! WHERE'S YOUR SHE-TURTLE?
SHE DITCHED ME FOR SOME MUSCLE-BOUND IDIOT!

THIS DOPE WOULDN'T KNOW VERMEER FROM VICHYSSOISE.
I'LL BET NOT.
HMPH. THE FOOL.

THE FIRST ONE'S A POWER RANGER.
I THINK THAT OTHER THING MAKES CHEESE.

I SEE YOU'VE GONE INTO THE DRY CLEANING BUSINESS NOW.
YEP.
DRY CLEANING BY HAWTHORNE

IS THERE REALLY A BIG NEED FOR THAT AMONG FISH?
WHO KNOWS.

IS THERE REALLY A NEED FOR ANY OF MY BUSINESSES?
DRY CLEANING BY

OR EVEN FOR YOU, COME TO THINK OF IT.
HUH?
DRY CLEANING BY

I'VE GOT A FEW ITEMS THAT I'D LIKE DRY CLEANED.
OKEY DOKE.
DRY CLEANING BY HAWTHORNE

AND SOME OF THESE THINGS ARE A LITTLE PRIVATE, IF YOU KNOW WHAT I MEAN.
DRY CLEANING BY

NATURALLY, WE EXERCISE COMPLETE CONFIDENTIALITY IN THESE MATTERS.
GOOD. THANKS.
DRY CLEANING BY

HEY! NO GUARANTEE ON THE SPIDERMAN UNDIES!

HOW'S BUSINESS?
ACTUALLY, IT'S TOO GOOD. I NEED AN EMPLOYEE.
DRY CLEANING BY

SAY, HOW WOULD YOU LIKE TO WORK FOR ME?
ME? I DON'T KNOW, HAWTHORNE.

SOMETHING LIKE THAT COULD RUIN OUR FRIENDSHIP.
I DON'T CONSIDER YOU A FRIEND.
DRY CLEANING BY

THEN I'M YOUR MAN!
GET TO WORK, JERK!
DRY CLEANING BY HAWTHORNE

HERE'S YOUR DRY CLEANING, FILLMORE.
YOU SHRANK MY SCARF!

NO. I DON'T THINK WE DID.
IT'S THE SIZE OF A TOWLETTE!

WHY WOULD I HAVE A SCARF THIS SIZE? IT'S ABSURD!
GOT ME!

WHY DO YOUR T-SHIRTS SAY "LADIES MAN" ON THEM? THAT'S ABSURDER!
THAT'S NOT A WORD!

WHAT DO YOU HAVE THERE?
MRS. ROBBINS' LATEST DRY CLEANING.
DRY CLEANING BY

THERE'S SOMETHING IN HER POCKET... OH MY, IT'S A MINI SPEAR GUN.
HOLY SCHMOLEY.
DRY CLEANING BY

AND THERE'S SOMETHING ELSE IN HERE.
WHAT IS IT?
DRY CLEANING BY

PICTURES OF US WITH TARGETS ON THEM.
LET'S GIVE HER 15% OFF.
DRY CLEANING BY

THIS DRY CLEANING BUSINESS IS NOT FOR ME. I HAVE TO FIND A WAY TO GET OUT WITHOUT LOSING MY INVESTMENT.
DRY CLEANING BY

MAYBE A DISGRUNTLED EMPLOYEE COULD BURN THE PLACE DOWN... YEAH... THEN I'LL COLLECT INSURANCE.
DRY CLEANING BY

BUT, I'M YOUR ONLY EMPLOYEE.
WOULD YOU CONSIDER YOURSELF DISGRUNTLED?
DRY CLEANING BY

NOPE. I'VE NEVER BEEN MORE GRUNTLED.
WELL GET OVER IT!
DRY CLEANING BY

I DON'T GET IT. HOW CAN AN UNDERWATER BUSINESS BURN TO THE GROUND? VERRRRY SUSPICIOUS.

FAIR ENOUGH. THEN WHY THE NEED TO PAY FOR AN UNDERWATER FIRE MARSHAL?

I WON'T TELL IF YOU WON'T.
SEE YOU AT POKER.

SHERMAN'S LAGOON

YOUR POEM DOESN'T RHYME.
A POEM DOESN'T HAVE TO RHYME.

THEN IT'S JUST A BUNCH OF WORDS.
FINE. THEN THAT'S WHAT I'M WORKING ON. A BUNCH OF WORDS.

YOU SHOULD WORK ON A POEM.
ISN'T THERE A BUFFET OPEN SOMEWHERE?

HERE YOU GO, GUYS. MEMBERSHIP FORMS FOR MY NEW HEALTH CLUB.

IT'S GONNA BE AN EXCLUSIVE, STATE-OF-THE-ART FACILITY.

SO, WHAT'RE THE CRITERIA FOR GETTING IN?
JUST FILL OUT THE FORM.

HOW DOES THAT MAKE IT EXCLUSIVE?
NO ILLITERATES.
I'M STUCK ON NO. 1.

SHERMAN! WELCOME TO MY NEW HEALTH CLUB.
THANKS, HAWTHORNE.

SO, WHAT DO YOU THINK?
LOOKS NICE.

THE NAME'S A LITTLE ODD, THOUGH.
WELL, THAT'S BECAUSE I'M THE ONLY ONE WORKING HERE...

... AND I LIKE A LONG LUNCH.
CAN'T ARGUE WITH THAT.
22-HOUR FITNESS

WOW! WHAT A HEALTH CLUB! WHAT MACHINE SHOULD I TRY FIRST?

TAKE YOUR PICK. WE'VE GOT IT ALL HERE AT 22-HOUR FITNESS. STAIRMASTERS, TREADMILLS, STATIONARY BIKES...

AND ALL THE MACHINES ARE TOP OF THE LINE.
OOH. I'M GONNA TRY THAT ONE.

THE VENDING MACHINE.
SPOT ME.
SNACKS

HOW WAS TODAY'S WORKOUT, FILLMORE?
TOUGH. I'M UP TO TEN POUNDS ON THE BENCH PRESS.
SQUIDOS

I DID ONE REP. PHEW!

ISN'T "REP" SHORT FOR "REPETITION"?
YEAH. SO?

IT'S NOT REALLY REPETITION IF YOU DO ONLY ONE.
I'LL DO ANOTHER ONE TOMORROW!

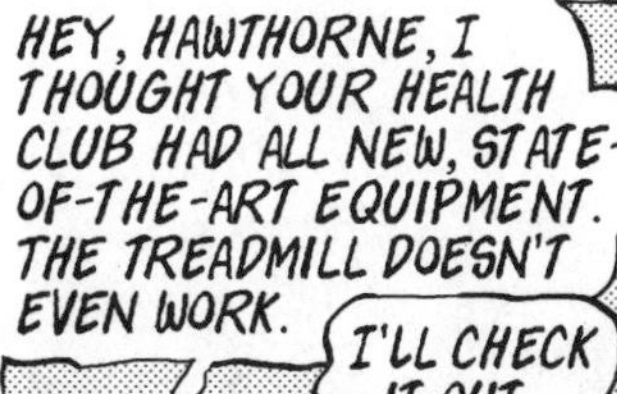
HEY, HAWTHORNE, I THOUGHT YOUR HEALTH CLUB HAD ALL NEW, STATE-OF-THE-ART EQUIPMENT. THE TREADMILL DOESN'T EVEN WORK.

I'LL CHECK IT OUT.
22-HOUR

PROBABLY SOMETHING TECHNICAL. THESE FANCY NEW MACHINES ARE TOO COMPLICATED.

LOOK. IT'S SMOKING.
LEMME TAKE A LOOK INSIDE.

WHEN'S THE BREAK OVER?
FIVE MORE MINUTES.

SHERMAN'S LAGOON

HERE AT MY NEW FITNESS CENTER WE HAVE NOTHING BUT THE LATEST IN EXERCISE TECHNOLOGY.
22-HOUR

WHAT'S THIS STRETCHY THING?
IT'S A RESISTANCE TRAINING DEVICE. STATE OF THE ART.
22-HOUR FITNE

IT LOOKS LIKE THE ELASTIC BAND FROM YOUR UNDERWEAR.
DON'T BE FOOLED BY THE SIMILARITY.
22-HOUR FITN

WHAT'S THIS LABEL THAT SAYS "TUESDAY"?
UH, WORKOUT REMINDER.
22-HOUR FITN

SAY, HAWTHORNE, IS THAT SOME NEW WORKOUT MACHINE?
UH, YEAH.
WRRRRRRRRR

IT EXERCISES THE, UH... DELTOIDS AND LATS.
OOH. NICE.

JUST GRAB THIS HANDLE, PUSH THE BUTTON, AND WORK IT BACK AND FORTH. FEEL THE BURN.
GOT IT.

WHY ARE YOU VACUUMING THE FITNESS CENTER?
QUIET, MEGAN. I'M IN THE ZONE.
WRRRRRRRR

I'VE COMPLETED A FULL WEEK OF DAILY WORKOUTS AT THE NEW HEALTH CLUB, MEGAN.
YEAH. SO?

CAN'T YOU NOTICE A DIFFERENCE?
NOT REALLY.

I'VE BEEN HITTING THE ABDOMINAL MACHINE PRETTY HARD.
STILL FEELS KIND OF SOFT.

THOSE ARE THE FLABDOMINALS. THE FLABS PROTECT THE ABS.
I'LL TAKE YOUR WORD FOR IT.

Sherman's Lagoon

THE HEALTH CLUB IS CLOSED? WHAT'S UP?
EVERYONE QUIT.
CLOSED

YOU WERE THE ONLY ONE WHO BELIEVED IN THIS PLACE.
SHOOT.

AND I WAS JUST ABOUT TO UPGRADE TO GOLD MEMBER STATUS.
CLOSED

WHAT WOULD THAT HAVE GOTTEN ME, ANYHOW?
THE CLEAN TOWEL.
CLOSED

DID YOU FIND ANYTHING GOOD AT THE GARAGE SALE, SHERMAN?
I BOUGHT THIS COOL STUFFED SWORDFISH.

AUGH!
WHAT IS IT?

I'VE SEEN THIS SWORDFISH BEFORE.

IT'S SALLY FROM MY BOOK CLUB!
I DIDN'T RECOGNIZE HER WITH HER MOUTH CLOSED.

I CAN'T BELIEVE IT. YOU COME HOME FROM A GARAGE SALE WITH A STUFFED SWORDFISH, AND IT TURNS OUT TO BE A FRIEND OF MINE.

SO, HOW 'BOUT WE HANG HER IN THE REC ROOM?
SHE WAS MY FRIEND! SHE NEEDS A PROPER RESTING PLACE!

SO, YOU WERE THINKING IN THE BEDROOM?
WE NEED TO BURY HER!

OKAY, GET A GRIP ON YOURSELF... YOU MUST BE HALUCINATING... SHERMAN GAVE SALLY A PROPER BURIAL. SHE COULDN'T BE HANGING ON FILLMORE'S WALL. THAT'S ABSURD. SHE'S...

SHERMAN! YOU WERE SUPPOSED TO GIVE MY FRIEND SALLY A PROPER BURIAL!
UH-OH.

YOU SOLD HER TO HAWTHORNE, WHO SOLD HER TO FILLMORE, WHO GAVE HER TO ERNEST!

I DON'T KNOW HOW I CAN EVER TRUST IN YOU AGAIN!

I'VE STILL GOT THE FIFTY BUCKS I MADE SELLING HER.
DINNER OUT COULD START THE HEALING.

AUGH!

IT BURNS! IT BURNS!

WHAT HAPPENED TO HIM?

HE ACCIDENTALLY ATE A VEGETABLE.
OOH. SHARK KRYPTONITE.

UH OH, SHARK IN THE BAR!!
RELAX, I'VE ALREADY EATEN.

GOOD. 'CUZ YOU DON'T KNOW HOW DIFFICULT IT IS BEING A LOBSTER.

SO SUCCULENT AND TASTY. EACH BITE TASTIER THAN THE PREVIOUS ONE.

MPHT.. HE TALKED ME INTO IT..
GOTTA KNOW WHEN TO SHUT UP.

SHERMAN'S LAGOON

SHERMAN, DOES THIS DRESS MAKE ME LOOK FAT?

THE DRESS ISN'T IMPORTANT, MEGAN, IT'S THE WOMAN WEARING IT.

THE FACT IS, YOU'RE BEAUTIFUL, AND I'M LUCKY TO BE MARRIED TO YOU.

YOU'RE MY SOUL MATE. YOU MAKE ME COMPLETE.

YOU'RE THE LIGHT OF MY LIFE. THE SUNSHINE IN MY HEART.

EVERY MORNING, WHEN I WAKE UP BY YOU, I THANK MY LUCKY STARS.

DO I LOOK THAT FAT?
HOW DO I LOVE THEE? LET ME COUNT THE WAYS.

HEY FAT BOY, I UNDERSTAND YOU HAD A LITTLE PARTY LAST NIGHT. WHY WASN'T I INVITED?

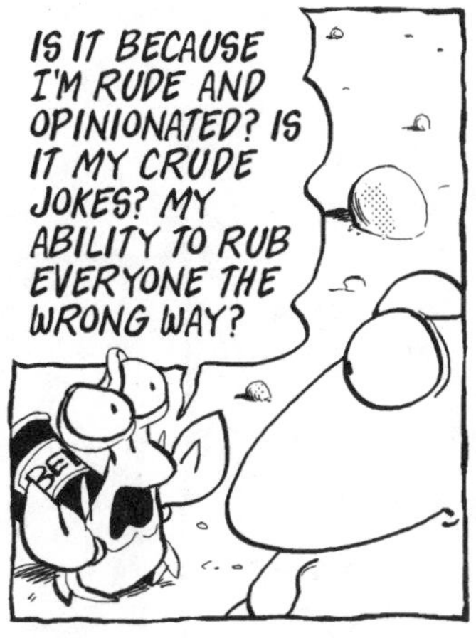
IS IT BECAUSE I'M RUDE AND OPINIONATED? IS IT MY CRUDE JOKES? MY ABILITY TO RUB EVERYONE THE WRONG WAY?

I GUESS I WOULDN'T HAVE INVITED ME EITHER.
SO YOU CAN SEE THE DILEMMA WE NEVER HAD.

SHERMAN, I'VE GOT AN EXCITING VACATION PLANNED FOR US!
SIGN ME UP!

WE'RE GOING TO THE "ALOHA" STATE!
NEBRASKA?
TRAVEL

TRAVEL

THAT'S THE "OMAHA" STATE.
RIGHT.
TRAVEL

SO WHY DID YOU CHOOSE HAWAII FOR OUR NEXT VACATION?

THE WARM WATER, THE NICE BEACHES, THE PALM TREES.
WE HAVE ALL THAT HERE.

LUAUS WITH HUGE ROASTED PIGS.
I'LL GET MY TRAVEL FORK.

SHERMAN'S LAGOON

WELL, WE'RE HERE, SHERMAN. HAWAII.
LET THE VACATION BEGIN.

THIS RESORT I BOOKED FOR US CATERS ESPECIALLY TO SHARKS.
CLUB

ALOHA, AND WELCOME TO CLUB SHARK. HERE ARE YOUR LEIS.

MMMM. SMELLS NICE.
OOH... CHUNKS OF HAM.

SHERMAN, I'M SO EXCITED ABOUT BEING IN HAWAII I DON'T KNOW IF I CAN SLEEP.

OOH!

WELL, SOMEBODY'S GETTING A LITTLE FRISKY. WE SHOULD GO ON AN ISLAND VACATION MORE OFTEN.
CLICK

SAYS HERE THERE'S QUITE A WILD PIG PROBLEM ON THE ISLAND.
AAAUGH!!

I SIGNED US UP FOR HULA DANCING LESSONS, SHERMAN.
MEGAN, I DON'T DANCE.

BUT, WE USED TO DANCE ALL THE TIME.
WHEN WE WERE DATING. WE'RE MARRIED NOW.

SO, THAT WAS A RUSE TO CLOSE THE DEAL. NOW WE CAN SHOW OUR TRUE SELVES, HUH?
SORT OF.

WELL, NOW THAT WE'RE MARRIED, I'M GOING TO GAIN 50 POUNDS.
HULA! SIGN ME UP!

OKAY, WE'VE LEARNED SOME HULA MOVES. WE'RE READY TO TELL A STORY.

SHERMAN, YOU GO FIRST... MEGAN, YOU INTERPRET.

OKAY, OKAY... GOT IT...

HEY! KEEP MY MOTHER OUT OF THIS!
IT'S MY STORY. THANK YOU.

OKAY, CLASS, SHERMAN IS GOING TO TELL US A STORY THROUGH HULA DANCING. I WANT TO SEE IF YOU CAN INTERPRET IT.

IT'S FUN TO STAY AT THE Y.M.C.A.
BINGO.

OKAY, MEGAN, ARE YOU READY TO TRY THE HULA?
YOU BET.

AND SHERMAN, THIS TIME YOU INTERPRET HER MOVES AND TRY TO FIGURE OUT WHAT STORY SHE'S TELLING.
ALRIGHTY.

UH HUH... UH, HUH...
HEY, WAIT...

I DID SO PUT THE SEAT BACK DOWN!
CHAPTER TWO...

WE FLUNKED OUR HULA DANCING CLASS.
WE DID?

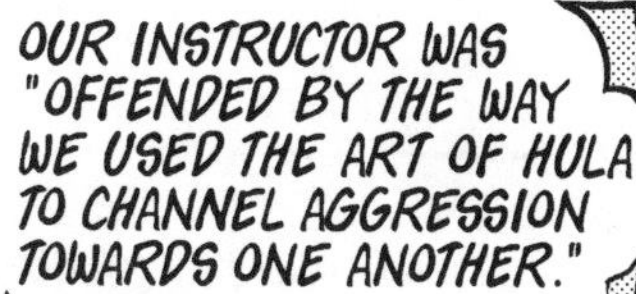
OUR INSTRUCTOR WAS "OFFENDED BY THE WAY WE USED THE ART OF HULA TO CHANNEL AGGRESSION TOWARDS ONE ANOTHER."

JUST FOR ONCE I WISH WE COULD PARTICIPATE IN AN ACTIVITY TOGETHER WITHOUT IT TURNING INTO A FIGHT.

I SIGNED US UP FOR SOMETHING ELSE AND YOU'RE GOING TO LIKE IT.
KICK BOXING?

NO VISIT TO HAWAII WOULD BE COMPLETE WITHOUT TRYING TO SURF.
YOU'RE GOING TO SURF?

YEAH. WHY NOT?
PADDLING AROUND UP THERE ON THE SURFACE MAKES YOU AN EASY TARGET. WHAT ABOUT SHARKS?

YOU'RE THE ONLY OTHER SHARK AROUND.
I CAN BE AN IMPULSIVE EATER.

LARGE, FROZEN DRINKS ARE AN ESSENTIAL PART OF ANY TROPICAL VACATION, SHERMAN.

AND THIS BAR CLAIMS TO SERVE THE BIGGEST ONES ON THE ISLAND.

YOUR FLAMING VOLCANO FOR TWO.
OOF!

WOW, THAT IS BIG.
LOOK. IT HAS A TIDE.

SHERMAN'S LAGOON

SHERMAN'S LAGOON

YOU'RE BACK.
YEP. OUR VACATION'S OVER.

BOY, IT SEEMED LIKE JUST YESTERDAY YOU GUYS LEFT.
THAT WAS 10 DAYS AGO, AND, BELIEVE ME, 10 DAYS IS NOT LONG ENOUGH.
TELL ME ABOUT IT.

THEY'RE BACK.
OUR VACATION'S OVER.

COOL COFFEE TABLE, HAWTHORNE.
YEAH, IT'S AN OLD SHIP'S DOOR. LOOK AT ALL THE WOODWORM HOLES. THIS SUCKER'S ANCIENT.

THIS IS PROBABLY WHERE SOME PIRATE TRIED TO OPEN IT WITH A HATCHET... HERE'S WHERE THE HINGES WERE RIPPED OUT.
PFT!

AND, JUST TO GIVE IT EVEN MORE OF A DISTRESSED LOOK, I POUNDED IT WITH THIS CHAIN.
NICE TOUCH.

USE A COASTER, FOR CRYING OUT LOUD!
SORRY.

HEY HAWTHORNE, I'M WORKING ON MY WILL. WHO SHOULD I LEAVE MY STEREO TO?
THAT OLD THING? NOBODY WANTS IT.

HOW ABOUT MY FLINTSTONES JELLY JAR COLLECTION?
RECYCLE IT. THEY COLLECT GLASS ON TUESDAYS.

WELL, THAT'S ABOUT EVERYTHING I OWN...
AT LEAST I CAN BE AN ORGAN DONOR.

WHO SHOULD I LEAVE THOSE TO?
ALPO.

SHERMAN'S LAGOON

I'VE DECIDED TO WRITE A BOOK.
THAT'S GREAT, MEGAN.

I'VE WATCHED MARTHA STEWART ENOUGH OVER THE YEARS. I'LL JUST FOLLOW HER LEAD.

WELL, NOBODY DOES IT LIKE MARTHA. IT'LL BE A GREAT BOOK.

WE ARE TALKING ABOUT INSIDER TRADING TIPS.
COOKING.

HAWTHORNE, I'M WRITING A COOKBOOK. CAN YOU GUYS PUBLISH IT?
SURE.
HAWTHORNE MEDIA

HOW BIG OF AN ADVANCE CAN YOU OFFER ME?

MEGAN, WE'RE JUST A TINY OPERATION. WE CAN'T OFFER UP ANY ADVANCES.
HAWTHORNE MEDIA

I'M THINKING OF DEVOTING AN ENTIRE CHAPTER TO HERMIT CRAB RECIPES.
I'M CHECKING PETTY CASH.
ORNE MEDIA

HEY, MEGAN, I HEAR YOU'RE WRITING A COOKBOOK.
YEP.

I'VE BEEN COOKING FOR 84 HOURS STRAIGHT TO GET THESE RECIPES RIGHT.
WOW.

SHERMAN'S BEEN A SAINT, STAYING UP WITH ME AND TESTING EVERYTHING.

SHERMAN? YOU ALRIGHT?
MEGAN! THE TURTLE SOUP'S TALKING TO ME!

SHERMAN'S LAGOON

SO, MEGAN, HOW'S THE COOKBOOK COMING?
WELL...

IT'S BECOMING TEDIOUS. I'M RUNNING LOW ON PATIENCE.

JUST FOCUS ON THE SENSE OF ACCOMPLISHMENT YOU'LL HAVE ONCE YOU'RE FINISHED.

WHAT HAVE YOU EVER FINISHED?
THIS THREE STOOGES MARATHON!

MEGAN, WE'RE ALMOST READY TO GO TO PRINT WITH YOUR COOKBOOK.
GREAT.
Hawthorne Media Enterprises
President/CEO/CFO

YOU'RE SURE ALL THESE RECIPES ARE LEGITIMATE?
OF COURSE!
Hawthorne Media Enterprises
President/CEO/CFO

ARE YOU IMPLYING THAT I GOT LAZY AND FILLED UP PAGES JUST TO MEET MY DEADLINE?
WELL...
Hawthorne Media Enterprises
President/CEO/CFO

...THIS RECIPE IS IDENTICAL TO THE ONE ON THE BOX OF CAPTAIN CRUNCH.
THEY GOT IT FROM ME!
Hawthorne Media Enterprises
CAP'N CRUNCH
President/CEO/CFO

MEGAN, I'M HAVING TROUBLE WITH YOUR "BEANS AND FRANKS" RECIPE.
BOOK SIGNING

OH MY. EVERY SELF-RESPECTING SHARK SHOULD KNOW HOW TO MAKE THAT.
I MANAGED TO FIND BEANS EASILY ENOUGH.

BUT I CAN'T FIND 3 HAIRLESS BEACH APES NAMED "FRANK."
THAT CAN BE TRICKY.
BOOK SIGNING

THERE'S AN EASIER VERSION ON PAGE 27.
"BEANS AND STEVES"?
BOOK SIGNING

SHERMAN'S LAGOON

YOU WANTED TO SEE ME?
MEGAN, WE HAVE TO PULL YOUR COOKBOOK.
Hawthorne Media Enterprises
President/CEO/CFO

TOO MANY COMPLAINTS ABOUT YOUR RECIPES. "UNSOPHISTICATED... SIMPLISTIC... TOO FATTENING... JUST PLAIN WEIRD..."
President/CEO/CFO

DID YOU TRY ANY OF THEM?
I TRIED YOUR "SUGAR SPRINKLED ON A STICK OF BUTTER," AND I MUST SAY, IT WAS ADDICTING.
President/CEO/CFO

AND, WHILE I PERSONALLY AM A FAN OF YOUR WORK...
WHAT ARE YOU HIDING BACK THERE?
Hawthorne Media Enterprises

ANCHOR!!

BONK!

WHOA NELLY, HE'S OUT COLD.
SHERMAN?

I'LL CHECK HIS PULSE.
I'LL CHECK HIS BREATHING.
I'LL CHECK HIS WALLET.

MEGAN, WE THINK SHERMAN BROKE HIS DORSAL FIN.
OH MY! WHAT HAPPENED?

WELL, WE WERE ALL SITTING AROUND TALKING, WHEN ALL OF A SUDDEN THIS HUGE ANCHOR...

HOLD THAT THOUGHT.

WE'RE BACK FROM COMMERCIAL.
NEVER DIE DURING OPRAH.

OH, SHERMAN, I CAME AS QUICKLY AS I COULD. ARE YOU OKAY?
WELL, THEY TOOK SOME X-RAYS.

AND?
GOOD NEWS AND BAD NEWS.

WHAT'S THE BAD NEWS?
MY DORSEL FIN IS BROKEN.

WHAT'S THE GOOD NEWS?
WE'VE LOCATED THE T.V. REMOTE.

OKAY, SHERMAN, JUST RING THE BELL IF YOU NEED ANYTHING.
THANKS, MEGAN.

DING DING DING
COMING!

DING DING DING
COMING AGAIN!

HOW'S SHERMAN'S BROKEN FIN?
BETTER. BUT NOW HE'S GOT A BELL UP HIS NOSE.

LOOK AT ALL THE BEACH APES IN THE WATER, AND I'M STUCK HERE IN THIS HOSPITAL BED! WHAT KIND OF SHARK AM I?
YOU'LL BE BACK SOON, CHAMP.

HEY, WAIT A MINUTE... DILL ... GARLIC... A LITTLE OREGANO.

I'M MISSING IT! THEY COME ONLY ONCE EVERY 5 YEARS!!

WHO?
THE PRE-SEASONED SWIM CLUB!

HOW'S THE HOSPITAL TREATING YOU, SHERMAN?
FINE. THANKS FOR VISITING.

AND, THANKS FOR THE FLOWERS.
BOY, WHAT A RACKET. I SHOULD BE IN THE FLOWER BIZ.

SO, DO THE DOCTORS THINK YOU'LL PULL THROUGH? YOU'RE NOT GOING TO CROAK ON US, ARE YOU?

I'M NOT GOING TO HAVE TO BLOW MORE MONEY ON FLOWERS, AM I?
I HOPE NOT.

SHERMAN, YOU'RE OUT OF THE HOSPITAL!
YEP. AND WITH A NEW ATTITUDE.

LIFE TO THE FULLEST. LIVE FOR TODAY. CARPE DIEM!

AHHHH.

THIS IS YOU LIVING FOR TODAY?
I DIDN'T MEAN **TODAY** TODAY.

WHAT'S WITH THE CAMERAS?
IT'S THE ANNUAL LAGOON FISHING TOURNAMENT.

OOOH! I'VE SEEN THAT HOST ON THE SATURDAY MORNING FISHING SHOWS.

YEP. NOTHING BUT THE BIG LEAGUERS HERE.

THAT IS ONE BIG MOUTHFUL OF CHEWING TOBACCO.
AND, SOMEHOW, SHE MAKES IT SEEM FEMININE.

SHERMAN'S LAGOON

WHAT SPORTS EVENT ARE YOU GUYS WATCHING NOW?
THE FISHING TOURNAMENT.

BUT, IT'S HAPPENING RIGHT HERE IN OUR LAGOON. WHY DON'T YOU JUST WATCH THE REAL THING?
YOU GET A BETTER VIEW OF THE ACTION ON TV.

BESIDES, IT'S DANGEROUS OUT THERE. THERE'RE HOOKS EVERYWHERE.

HERE ON THE COUCH IT'S SAFE.
ALRIGHT! WHO ORDERED THE PIZZA?

LOOK, IT'S BUBBA MCGUIRE. HE'S WON THIS FISHING TOURNAMENT THREE TIMES IN A ROW.

HE'S GOT ONE ON THE LINE NOW.

WHOA NELLY! LANDED IT WITH ONE HAND.
THE STRENGTH, THE SKILL.
BUBBA DOESN'T LIKE TO PUT HIS BEER DOWN.

WHOA, LOOK! SOMEBODY HOOKED A HUGE ONE.

THIS COULD BE THE TROPHY FISH OF THE TOURNAMENT.

IT APPEARS TO BE ATTACKING THE BOAT... I'VE NEVER SEEN ANYTHING LIKE IT!

THAT'S NO ORDINARY SHARK.
RED MAN

THAT'S MY WIFE.

SHERMAN, THOSE MEAN FISHERMEN WERE REELING ME IN AND YOU JUST SAT THERE AND WATCHED IT ON TV!

YOU LOOKED LIKE YOU WERE HANDLING YOURSELF ALRIGHT, MEGAN.
LUCKY FOR YOU THE LINE BROKE.

I THOUGHT THAT STEEL FISHING LINE WAS SUPPOSED TO HOLD 800 POUNDS.
WELL, DON'T ASK ME. IT JUST SNAPPED... IT MUST'VE BEEN DEFECTIVE

SAYS RIGHT HERE ON MY DRIVER'S LICENSE I'M ONLY 725 POUNDS.
MUST BE TRUE.

THE FISHING TOURNAMENT IS OVER, AND IT APPEARS THE OFFICIAL CASUALTY COUNT IS TWENTY-FIVE FISH. HERE'S THE LIST.

FILLMORE WOULD LIKE TO SAY SOMETHING IN MEMORY OF OUR COMRADES.
AHEM

TWENTY-FIVE BRAVE SOULS HAVE PAID THE ULTIMATE PRICE...
SNIFF

I ATE THREE OF THESE GUYS.
TWENTY-TWO BRAVE SOULS...

GOOD HEAVENS! WHERE'D YOU FIND THAT NECKLACE, SHERMAN?
IN A TREASURE CHEST. WHY?

THAT'S THE INFAMOUS SOCK-IT-TO-ME NECKLACE. IT'S CURSED.
NONSENSE.

I'M SERIOUS. BAD THINGS HAPPEN TO WHOMEVER TOUCHES IT.
CURSE SCHMURSE.

YOU'VE JUST DEVELOPED TED KOPPEL HAIR.
NOT BUYING IT.

Sherman's Lagoon

MEGAN, I GOT YOU THIS NECKLACE FROM A TREASURE CHEST.
OH, SHERMAN, IT'S BEAUTIFUL.

IT'S NOT THAT FAMOUS CURSED NECKLACE THAT EVERYONE IS TALKING ABOUT, IS IT?

KABOOM!

WOW. YOUR BEST SOUFFLÉ YET.
PRACTICE MAKES PERFECT.

HEY, MEGAN, BEAUTIFUL NECKLACE.
THANK YOU, HAWTHORNE.

SHERMAN FOUND IT IN A TREASURE CHEST AND GAVE IT TO ME.

SOME PEOPLE SAY IT'S CURSED. I THINK IT'S A BUNCH OF HOOEY.

NICE TAIL.
I KNEW THE WORKOUTS WOULD PAY OFF.

MEGAN, I THINK THAT NECKLACE I GAVE YOU MIGHT REALLY BE CURSED. MAYBE I SHOULD GET RID OF IT.

I WOULDN'T WANT ANYTHING BAD HAPPENING TO YOU.
DON'T EVEN THINK ABOUT IT, SHERMAN.

IN FACT, I GOT A CALL TODAY WITH SOME GOOD NEWS.

MOM'S VISITING NEXT WEEK.
IT'S AFFECTING ALL OF US!

GREAT DINNER, MEGAN.
THANK YOU, DEAR.

AND SEE, NOTHING BAD HAPPENED. THE NECKLACE YOU GAVE ME ISN'T CURSED AFTERALL.

WELL, I'M TIRED. I THINK I'LL TURN IN.

MAYBE I UNDERCOOKED THE SALMON.
I DON'T THINK THAT WOULD RESULT IN COW FACE.

SHERMAN, YOU'RE RIGHT. THIS THING'S CURSED. GET RID OF IT.
IT'S FOR THE BEST.

NO ONE WILL FIND IT WAY OUT HERE.

HMPH!

AUGH! I'M HIDEOUS!
BOB?

WRITING ANOTHER BUSINESS PLAN, HAWTHORNE?
YEP.

WHAT IS IT?
NOT SURE YET. IT'S STILL IN THE CONCEPTUAL PHASE. GOT ANY SUGGESTIONS?

THE TRICK IS TO FIND SOMETHING THAT YOU'RE PASSIONATE ABOUT. THEN, IF YOU CAN MAKE MONEY AT IT, THAT'S ICING ON THE CAKE.

WHAT ARE YOU PASSIONATE ABOUT?
MAKING MONEY.

SHERMAN'S LAGOON

HERE YOU GO, BOYS. 10% OFF COUPONS TO MY NEW ONE-HOUR PHOTO BUSINESS.

I'M HERE FOR ALL OF YOUR QUALITY PHOTO NEEDS.
WHAT'S THE FINE PRINT?

OFFER GOOD FROM 2:00 A.M. TO 2:15 A.M. TUESDAY...

WHO WOULD DROP OFF THEIR PICTURES AT THAT HOUR?
DOESN'T MATTER. WE'RE CLOSED ANYWAY.

THERE'S A PROBLEM WITH THE PHOTOS YOU DEVELOPED.
ONE-HOUR PHOTO

I DROPPED OFF A ROLL OF FILM I TOOK OF MY GRANDSON'S BIRTHDAY PARTY.
YEAH?

THESE AREN'T EVEN FOLKS I KNOW. AND LOOK AT THIS ONE...
PHOTO

SOME WEIRDO IN NINJA TURTLE UNDERWEAR.
HEY!
ONE-HOUR PHOTO

GOOD HEAVENS! A U.F.O.!
CLICK!

HAWTHORNE! BE VERY CAREFUL! THIS IS HISTORY MAKING FILM!
PHOTO

ALL OF OUR FILM IS GIVEN THE SAME FIRST-CLASS TREATMENT.

AS YOU CAN SEE, I GOT RID OF THAT OBJECT BLOCKING THE MOUNTAIN.
AUGH!

I'M A PROFESSIONAL PHOTOGRAPHER! YOU'VE RUINED THIS ENTIRE ROLL OF FILM!
ONE-HOUR PHOTO
15 Years in Business

I'M GOING TO HAVE TO RE-SHOOT THIS WHOLE FAMILY PORTRAIT!
PHOTO
15 Years in

SORRY... WE'RE KINDA NEW AT THIS.
PHOTO
15 Years in

YOUR SIGN SAYS "15 YEARS IN BUSINESS"!
YEAH, BUT NOT IN THIS BUSINESS.
15 Years

I TOOK MY ROLL OF FILM TO HAWTHORNE'S NEW PHOTO SHOP, AND THE PRINTS HE GAVE ME BACK ARE ACTUALLY YOURS... THEY'RE OF YOU WORKING ON YOUR...

MY WHAT!? MY INTERPRETIVE DANCE MOVES? YES, I ADMIT IT!

I WAS GONNA SAY WORKING ON YOUR JIGSAW PUZZLE.
OH.

BUT SINCE YOU OPENED THIS CAN OF WORMS...
I'LL GET THE HUSH-MONEY JAR.

NO MORE ONE-HOUR PHOTO BUSINESS?
NAH. EVERYONE WAS GETTING TOO UPSET.

YOU SHOULDN'T START A BUSINESS KNOWING NOTHING ABOUT IT.

ESPECIALLY WHEN IT INVOLVES REALLY PERSONAL STUFF.

BUT I'M FEELING GOOD ABOUT MY NEW VENTURE.
DO YOU DO FETISHES?
PSYCHOLOGIST IN A BOX

SHERMAN'S LAGOON

HEY, LOOK! THE ANTIQUES TRAVEL SHOW IS COMING HERE.
WHAT'S THAT?

IT'S THIS WONDERFUL SHOW ON PBS ABOUT ANTIQUES.

YEAH. I WATCHED THAT ONCE.
YOU WATCHED PBS?
SURE.

WAS YOUR CABLE SERVICE OUT?
COULDN'T REACH THE REMOTE.

MEGAN, THE ANTIQUES TRAVEL SHOW IS COMING HERE.
I HEARD.

I THINK I'LL TAKE DOWN THIS WEDDING DRESS FROM MY MOTHER.

WE'VE PUT UP WITH THIS MOTH BALL-SCENTED OLD RAG FOR YEARS. MAYBE IT'S TIME TO GET RID OF IT.

THE MOTHER OR THE DRESS?
WE'LL DISCUSS THAT CRACK LATER.

WHAT HAVE YOU BROUGHT TO US?
A SWORD.
ANTIQUES TRAVEL SHOW

MILITARY EQUIPMENT CAN BE QUITE VALUABLE.
HERE IT IS.
ANTIQUES TRAVEL SHOW

THIS IS JUST A COCKTAIL SWORD... WITH THE LITTLE ONION STILL ON IT.
ANTIQUES TRAVEL SHOW

ARE YOU JUST TRYING TO GET YOURSELF ON TELEVISION?
YOU OWE ME FIVE BUCKS, ERNEST!
ANTIQUES TRAVEL SHOW

ARE YOU KIDDING ME? IT'S NOT WORTH A FORTUNE?
WELL, I MUST ADMIT, IT'S IN FINE SHAPE.
ANTIQUES TRAVEL SHOW

BUT, FAMILY HEIRLOOM OR NOT, IT'S STILL A WHOOPIE CUSHION... ANYTHING ELSE?

ANTIQUES TRAVEL SHOW

I'VE GOT THIS ART DECO FAKE VOMIT I'VE BEEN RESTORING.
NEXT!!
ANTIQUES TRAVEL SHOW

WEREN'T YOU ON OUR SHOW RECENTLY?
OH, NO. PROBABLY ANOTHER SHARK.
ANTIQUES TRAVEL SHOW

AND, YOU'RE NOT JUST HERE TO GET ON T.V.?
OF COURSE NOT.
ANTIQUES TRAVEL SHOW

FINE. WHAT'S IN THE BAG?
OH, I DUNNO... HOW ABOUT...
ANTIQUES TRAVEL SHOW

A RAINBOW WIG!
GET OUT!
ANTIQUES TRAVEL SHOW

WHEN'S OUR SEGMENT GOING TO AIR ON ANTIQUE TRAVEL SHOW?
NEVER!

THIS WAS THE WORST STOP WE'VE EVER MADE. NONE OF YOU DESERVES TO BE ON TELEVISION!

T.V. PERSONALITY EATEN BY SHARK.
SHOULD GET HIM ON THE NEWS.

SHERMAN'S LAGOON

WHAT'S UP WITH SHERMAN PLAYING CHESS WITH THE GIANT SQUID?

THEY'VE DECIDED TO MATCH WITS INSTEAD OF FIGHTING THIS TIME.
THIS WON'T LAST LONG.

AUGH!

OOH! QUEEN'S BISHOP TO LEFT NOSTRIL!
WELL PLAYED!

LOT OF PRESSURE BEING A SHARK.
HOW'S THAT?

WELL, JUST OUR NICKNAME... "PHILOSOPHERS OF THE DEEP."
NOBODY CALLS YOU THAT.

SUPPOSE WE COULD START?
NOT ON MY WATCH.

HEY, WHAT ARE YOU GUYS DOING?
I'M GONNA TEACH CLAYTON SPORTS.

WE'LL START WITH TOSSING THE BASEBALL AROUND.

WE ONLY HAVE TWO GLOVES, SO I'LL BE CATCHER AND YOU CAN BE PITCHER.

THAT KID'S IN TROUBLE.
DESTINED FOR MATH CLUB.

Sherman's Lagoon

SHERMAN'S LAGOON

SHERMAN, I THINK WE SHOULD DO SOMETHING RISKY.
LIKE WHAT?

WE SHOULD MAKE A TRIP TO THE BERMUDA TRIANGLE.
OOOH.

YOU KNOW, IF YOU REALLY WANT TO TAKE A RISK...
MORE OF YOUR HOMEMADE CHEESES?

THIS ONE'S A SWISS-CHEDDAR HYBRID.
SWEDDAR?

HERE YOU GO, BOYS. INVITES TO MY OBSERVATORY OPENING.

"COME EXPLORE THE WONDERS OF THE PLANETS, STARS, AND THE MOON."

HMMM.
WHAT?

WHAT DOES ONE WEAR TO A MOONING?
OBVIOUSLY NOT PANTS.

SHERMAN, YOU CAME TO HAVE A PEEK AT THE HEAVENS THROUGH MY SUPER-TELESCOPE?
YEAH. I LOVE SCIENCE.

WELL, GO AHEAD. KNOCK YOURSELF OUT, GALILEO.
ALL RIGHT.

HMMMM... HMMMM... OH MY! THERE IT IS! IT'S SPECTACULAR UP CLOSE! THE COLORS, THE LAYERS... (SNIFF) IT'S... BEAUTIFUL.

WHAT DID YOU FIND? A PLANET?
THE NEW MEATBALL SANDWICH AT SUBWAY.

MEGAN? YOU'RE INTERESTED IN ASTRONOMY?
NOT EXACTLY.
MAP

I'VE GOT THE COORDINATES TO MARTHA STEWART'S HOUSE... MAY I TAKE A PEEK AT MY HERO?
GO FOR IT.

OH MY! THERE SHE IS IN HER KITCHEN! LOOK AT HER USE THAT RUBBER SPATULA! WHIP IT, MARTHA! WHIP IT GOOD!
MAP

MASHED POTATOES?
CLEANING STAFF.

I WANT TO USE YOUR SUPER TELESCOPE TO OBSERVE THE HEAVENLY BODIES.
GOOD FOR YOU, HAWTHORNE.

EVERYONE ELSE IS INTERESTED IN STUPID STUFF.
AMATEURS.

OKAY, LET'S GET YOU SET UP. WHAT WOULD YOU LIKE TO SEE? A STAR? A PLANET?
A STAR.

POLARIS? SIRIUS? BETELGEUSE ?
PAMELA ANDERSON.

MOVE IT, FILLMORE. IT'S MY TURN TO USE THE SUPER TELESCOPE. IT'S MEAT DELIVERY DAY AT THE DELI. I WATCH.

TOUGH. I'M TRYING TO FIND A SHAKESPEARE FESTIVAL IN OREGON.

THAT'S STUPID. YOU CAN'T HEAR A PLAY THROUGH THE TELESCOPE!
BUT I CAN LIP READ!

DELI MEATS DON'T TALK AT ALL!
THEY SPEAK TO ME!!

SHERMAN, I'VE MADE A REMARKABLE DISCOVERY WITH MY SUPER TELESCOPE.
WHAT'S THAT?

IT'S A NEW PLANET BEYOND OUR SOLAR SYSTEM... AND, GET THIS... IT'S IDENTICAL TO EARTH IN EVERY WAY.
NO WAY! LEMME SEE.

HMPH.

YOU DON'T SEEM TO BE IMPRESSED.
OUR FLORIDA'S BIGGER.

STILL WATCHING THAT NEW PLANET THROUGH YOUR SUPER TELESCOPE?
YEP.

I'VE BEEN STUDYING THEIR SHARKS THIS MORNING.
REALLY? THEY HAVE SHARKS?

THEY'RE SMARTER THAN EARTH SHARKS.
HOW SO?

THEY DON'T EAT LICENSE PLATES.
HOW DO THEY GET THEIR IRON?

SHERMAN TELLS ME YOU'VE DISCOVERED A NEW PLANET.
YEP.

IDENTICAL TO EARTH, ONLY SLIGHTLY SMARTER.
REALLY? LIKE HOW?

WELL, THEY'RE MORE ADVANCED IN THE MUSIC INDUSTRY, FOR EXAMPLE.

BETTER ARTISTS?
THEIR CD'S CAN BE OPENED WITHOUT A MACHETE.

SO, TELL ME MORE ABOUT THIS NEW PLANET YOU'VE DISCOVERED, ERNEST.

WHY DO YOU THINK THEY'RE SO MUCH SMARTER THAN US?
THEIR INHABITANTS SEEM TO READ AN AWFUL LOT.

HEY, WE EARTHLINGS READ PLENTY!

THEY DO IT OUTSIDE OF THE BATHROOM.
BUT, THAT'S WHERE THE TV IS.

SHERMAN, YOU'VE BEEN SPENDING A LOT OF TIME LOOKING THROUGH THE TELESCOPE AT THIS NEW PLANET ERNEST DISCOVERED.
UNGH.

IT'S FASCINATING, MEGAN. IT'S A CULTURE JUST LIKE EARTH IN ALMOST EVERY WAY. THEY HAVE CITIES AND ROADS AND BUILDINGS.

HE USED TO SPEND HIS ENTIRE DAY WATCHING TV SPORTS...

AT LEAST THIS IS A LITTLE MORE INTELLECTUAL.
TOUCHDOWN!

WHY AREN'T YOU OVER AT ERNEST'S PLAYING WITH HIS SUPER TELESCOPE?

I'VE DECIDED I CAN'T DEVOTE THE TIME TO ASTRONOMY THAT I WOULD LIKE TO, SO I'VE GIVEN IT UP.

I HAVE TOO MANY INTELLECTUAL PURSUITS AS IT IS. I'M SPREADING MYSELF TOO THIN.

YOU MEAN, IT WAS EATING INTO NAP TIME.
I NEED MY BEAUTY SLEEP!

SHERMAN'S LAGOON

HI MEGAN. WHERE'S SHERMAN TODAY?
OH, HE'S A LITTLE UNDER THE WEATHER.

YOU KNOW MEN. THEY THINK THEY'RE SO MUCH WORSE THAN THEY REALLY ARE.

I FEEL BAD GOING OUT. BUT, HE'S GOT A COUPLE OF BUDDIES CHECKING UP ON HIM.

UHHH... LOOKS LIKE HE'S UP TO 350 DEGREES.
I SAY WE START BASTING.

WHERE'D THE BABY COME FROM?
WHAH!

MEGAN, COME ON. AT YOUR AGE? I THOUGHT YOU KNEW THIS STUFF.

THE REPRODUCTIVE PROCESS IS A MIRACLE OF NATURE. IT STARTS WHEN A...

I MEAN, HOW DID IT GET ON OUR DOORSTEP?!
YOU'RE JUMPING WAY AHEAD.

HOW IN THE WORLD DID THIS BABY END UP ON OUR DOORSTEP?

MAYBE THE STORK PAID US A VISIT.

STORKS DON'T BRING BABY FISH.

STORKS EAT BABY FISH.
MAYBE HE FORGOT HIS LUNCH.

OKAY, MEGAN, I THINK I'VE GOT THIS DIAPERING THING FIGURED OUT.

THIS GOES HERE, AND THEN FOLDS THIS WAY...

THEN A TUCK HERE AND HERE... AND THIS FASTENS TO THIS.

THERE. DID I FORGET ANYTHING?
EYEHOLES.

WHATCHA DOIN', SHERMAN?
WATCHING A LITTLE EDUCATIONAL TV.

I DON'T MIND TAKING A LITTLE TIME OUT OF MY BUSY DAY TO HELP THE LITTLE POOPER LEARN.

DON'T YOU WATCH SESAME STREET EVERY DAY AROUND THIS TIME?
WELL, EXCUSE MY THIRST FOR KNOWLEDGE!

SHERMAN, I'M BACK WITH THE BABY FORMULA.
IT'S OKAY. I FINALLY GOT HIM TO EAT.

GREAT. WHAT DID THE TRICK?
A BURRITO AND A DR. PEPPER.

TELL ME YOU'RE KIDDING.
UM, NO.

SAY, DO YOU HEAR THAT RUMBLING?
HE'S GONNA BLOW!

SHERMAN'S LAGOON

HE WON'T STOP CRYING. WHAT DO I DO?
DON'T YOU HAVE SOME MOTHERING INSTINCT THAT KICKS IN?
WHAH!

"MOTHERING." GOOD CALL, SHERMAN.

UH, HUH... OKAY, THANKS.

MOTHER'S COMING RIGHT OVER.
WHAH!
WHAH!

CHARLIE, THERE YOU ARE!
DA DA.

HE WANDERED OFF IN THE GROCERY STORE. I'VE BEEN GOING CRAZY LOOKING FOR HIM.

I CAN NEVER THANK YOU ENOUGH. I HOPE HE WASN'T TOO MUCH TROUBLE.
NAH. HE'S BEEN A DELIGHT. TAKE CARE.

AAAHHH...

REGISTERED LETTER FOR YOU.
OOH! WHO FROM?

IT'S FROM A FERGUS MACSHERMAN.
FERGUS MACSHERMAN?

SOUNDS KIND OF... YOU KNOW...

MADE-UP FOR A COMEDY BIT?
I WAS GOING TO SAY "SCOTTISH."

SO, WHO'S THIS FERGUS MACSHERMAN, AND WHY IS HE SENDING YOU A REGISTERED LETTER?
FERGUS IS MY GREAT UNCLE IN SCOTLAND.

OR WAS... HE JUST PASSED AWAY, AND HE LEFT ME A LOCH IN HIS WILL.

A LOCK? WHO LEAVES SOMEBODY A LOCK? DID HE LEAVE YOU A KEY, TOO?

IF YOU LOOK IN PANEL TWO, I CLEARLY SAID "LOCH" WITH AN "H."
RIGHT.

I SUPPOSE YOU'LL BE WANTING ME AS YOUR HEAD CRAB FOR YOUR NEW LOCH.
HUH?

OH, SURE, ALL YOUR BETTER LOCHS IN SCOTLAND HAVE CRAB MANAGEMENT.

AND, WHAT WOULD YOU DO?
YOU KNOW, DAY-TO-DAY OPERATIONS. BIG DECISIONS. THINGS LIKE THAT.

THEN, WHAT WOULD I DO?
LET'S SEE. I'VE GOT AN OPENING IN HOUSEKEEPING.

MEGAN, I THINK WE SHOULD MOVE TO THE LOCH IN SCOTLAND THAT I INHERITED.
WHAT?
WOMAN CARNIVORE

LEAVE THIS TROPICAL PARADISE AND ALL IT HAS TO OFFER?

I FEEL PRETTY, SO PRETTY... LA LA LA!

I GUESS WE COULD CHECK IT OUT.
THAT'S ALL I'M SAYING.

SHERMAN'S LAGOON

WHY ARE YOU WEARING A SKIRT?
IT'S A **KILT**. KILTS ARE **NOT** SKIRTS. KILTS ARE MANLY.

LONG AGO, BIG, HAIRY-CHESTED WARRIORS ARMED WITH SWORDS THE SIZE OF LAMP POSTS WORE KILTS.

I THINK I SAW ONE OF THOSE HAIRY KILT WOMEN ON JERRY SPRINGER ONE TIME.
IT'S **MAN'S** GARB. IT'S FOR **MEN**.

SO, YOU GOT YOURSELF A KILT.
I'VE JUST INHERITED A LOCH IN SCOTLAND. I HAVE TO LOOK THE PART.

FUNKY LOOKING PLAID.
IT'S CALLED A TARTAN.

YOUR TARTAN SAYS A LOT ABOUT YOU. IT'S WHO YOU ARE.

WHAT TARTAN IS THIS?
WAL-MART.

WE'RE ALL PACKED AND READY TO GO.
WHAT'S IN THAT CASE?

MY BAGPIPES. IF I'M GOING TO LIVE IN A REAL SCOTTISH LOCH, I'LL NEED TO KNOW HOW TO JAM ON THE PIPES WHEN REQUESTED.

WHERE ON EARTH DID YOU GET BAGPIPES?
WELL, I SORTA HAD TO MAKE THEM.

HOW DO YOU MAKE THEM?
PUFFER FISH AND A STRAW.
I'VE GOT A LAWYER.

HERE WE ARE, MEGAN. OUR VERY OWN SCOTTISH LOCH. THANKS TO UNCLE FERGUS.

ARE YOU WITH THE ESTATE OF FERGUS MACSHERMAN?

AYE. I'M THE NEW OWNER OF LOCH LEIGHNEACHTP. AND YOU ARE?
BILL...
WELL, BILL...

I HOPE WE CAN BECOME GREAT FRIENDS AND NEIGHBORS.

BILL COLLECTOR.
I'M GONNA CHANGE MY INITIAL ANSWER.

SHERMAN! WELCOME TO SCOTLAND!
NESSIE! GREAT TO SEE YOU AGAIN!

AND IT'S GREAT TO BE OUT ON THE LINKS WITH YOU... IF I REMEMBER RIGHT, YOU HAVE A PRETTY MEAN GAME.
AH, WELL, YOU KNOW...

WHACK!

ERE YA GONNA YAP OR ERE YA GINNA PLAY?
YEP, PRETTY MEAN ALL RIGHT.

SHERMAN, THIS WEATHER IN SCOTLAND IS DEPRESSING.

LET'S WATCH THE FORECAST. MAYBE IT'S GOING TO IMPROVE.
RAINY AGAIN ALL DAY TODAY.

BUT LOOK FOR CHANGES THIS EVENING...
HERE WE GO!

...WHEN IT'LL BE DARK AND RAINY. HA HA HA!
I HATE WILLARD SCOTTISH.

Sherman's Lagoon

I JUST LEARNED MY FIRST TUNE ON THE BAGPIPES, MEGAN. WANNA HEAR IT?
FIRE AWAY.

DOESN'T THAT SOUND STIR YOUR EMOTIONS?
UMMM... NOT MINE.

BUT I'M SURE SOMEWHERE OUT THERE A MOOSE IS RUTTING.
MORE PRACTICE.

WHY IS THAT GUY TOSSING A TELEPHONE POLE?

IT'S A CABER TOSSING CONTEST, MEGAN. APPARENTLY, THIS IS A POPULAR SPORT HERE IN SCOTLAND.

HUA!

WUMP!
UNGH!

WELL, NOW WE KNOW WHAT A SCOTSMAN WEARS UNDER HIS KILT.
YOO HOO. COVER YOURSELF.

NO TRIP TO SCOTLAND WOULD BE COMPLETE WITHOUT TRYING THE HIGHLAND MALT WHISKY.

TELL ME, WHY DO THE SCOTS LIKE THEIR WHISKY SO MUCH?

A DRAM O' WHISKY A DAY WILL KEEP YA WARM INSIDE, AND YOU'LL DIE AT A RIPE OLD AGE...

...AND YOU'LL LOOK GOOD FOR SEVERAL YEARS AFTER THAT.
WHAT THE HECK.

SHERMAN, WE HAVE TO BE BACK HOME BY TOMORROW.
THIS IS SUDDEN. WHY?
LIVING

I LEFT SOMETHING IN THE OVEN.
BUT WE'VE BEEN HERE A WEEK.

YEAH, WELL, IT'S MY MOTHER'S FAMOUS SQUID CASSEROLE.
LIVING

THE RECIPE CALLS FOR 8 DAYS.
THAT WOMAN DOESN'T COOK, SHE INCINERATES.
LIVING

HERE YOU GO. A V.I.P. PASS TO MY CASINO GRAND OPENING.
V.I.P.?

THAT'S RIGHT. ONLY MY INNER CIRCLE GETS THESE BABIES. RED CARPET TREATMENT.

HAWTHORNE, I'M TOUCHED. I'M HONORED.

HEY! WHATS-YER-FACE! I GOT A V.I.P. PASS FOR YOU!
A LITTLE LESS HONORED.

SHERMAN, MEGAN! WELCOME BACK. AND THANKS FOR COMING TO MY CASINO GRAND OPENING.

WE'VE GOT BLACK JACK, CRAPS, SLOTS, ROULETTE... WHAT'S YOUR PLEASURE?

OOH! WHAT'S THAT BIG ONE BACK THERE THAT'S ALL LIGHTED UP?

THAT'S A TELEVISION.
CAN'T LOSE THERE.

Sherman's Lagoon

MEGAN, SLOT MACHINES ARE CHUMP CHANGE. IF YOU WANNA MAKE REAL MONEY, PLAY A MAN'S GAME... POKER.

DING DING
DING DING
WOOOOO
WOOOOO

COULD I GET A HAND HERE?
STAY PUT. YOU MIGHT BE GOOD LUCK.

RED 23. YOU LOSE.
DO-OVERS.

THIS IS A CASINO. THERE AREN'T ANY DO-OVERS. YOU HAVE TO PUT OUT MORE MONEY.

BUT I GIVE YOU MULLIGANS IN GOLF.
A LOT MORE THAN YOU KNOW ABOUT.

I HATE THESE TOUGH CASINO DECISIONS.
WHAT'S UP?

WELL, I'M AT SEVENTEEN. WHAT SHOULD I DO?

I SAY HIT IT.
YOU SURE?

WHY NOT? IT'S ALL YOU CAN EAT.
OKAY. EIGHTEEN SHRIMP IT IS.

YOU THE OWNER OF DIS HERE CASINO?
YEAH. WHO ARE YOU?

NEVER MIND WHO I AM. I WAS SENT HERE TO TELL YOUSE DAT WE WANT 30% OF THE ACTION.
IN YOUR DREAMS, SOPRANO BOY... TWENTY, FORTY, SIXTY...

WE CAN MAKE YOUR LIFE VERY UNCOMFORTABLE.
YEAH YEAH... 100... 200...

MAYBE I WON'T HAVE THE PICKLED EGG.
THAT LOOKS VERY UNCOMFORTABLE.
Restauran

NO MOBFISH ARE GOING TO TAKE CONTROL OF MY CASINO. I'M NOT AFRAID OF THEM.

HMPH. WHY IS THERE A LUMP IN MY BED?

AUGH!

MEGAN WAS SNORING. CAN I SLEEP HERE?
GET OUT!

LISTEN, I TOLD YOU, MOBFISH, I WON'T GIVE IN TO YOU!
CASINO HAWTHORNE

I SUPPOSE YOU'RE CARRYING SOME KIND OF WEAPON IN THAT VIOLIN CASE.
YEP.

YOU'VE GOT ONE MORE CHANCE TO ACCEPT OUR.... UH... PROPOSAL.
NO WAY!

OKAY! OKAY! STOP PLAYING YANNI!
THAT'S WHAT I THOUGHT.

SHERMAN'S LAGOON

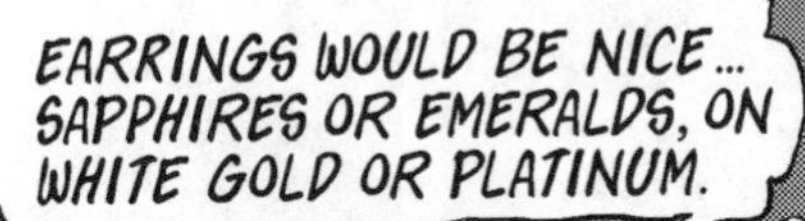

HEY, HAWTHORNE, WHAT HAPPENED TO YOUR CASINO?
HAD TO SHUT THE DOORS. BANKRUPT. KAPOOT.
CLOS

I DIDN'T THINK CASINOS COULD LOSE MONEY.
NEITHER DID I. I EVEN HIRED A CONSULTANT WHO HELPED ME CHEAT THE CUSTOMERS.

WE HAD THE ROULETTE WHEEL RIGGED, THE CARDS STACKED. WE WERE MAKING A TON OF DOUGH.

THEN HE STOLE IT ALL!
JUST WHEN YOU THINK YOU CAN TRUST SOMEBODY.

I'M GETTING WORRIED ABOUT THORNTON. MAYBE WE SHOULD GO LOOKING FOR HIM.
WE?

SURE. YOU AND I ON THE ROAD TOGETHER.
THAT'S A HORRIBLE IDEA.

THE MERE THOUGHT OF IT MAKES ME PHYSICALLY ILL.

SO, IT'S SETTLED. WE LEAVE TOMORROW.
LOOK. A HIVE.

READY TO WANDER THE OPEN SEAS IN SEARCH OF OUR BUDDY, THORNTON?
YEP. LET'S GO.

I'VE GOT ROAD TRIP ESSENTIALS... A MAP, A MOBILE PHONE, AND EMERGENCY CASH.

GOOD. I BROUGHT THE MUNCHIES.

THERE'S ONE SKITTLE IN THERE.
OKAY, THEN I BROUGHT THE "MUNCH."

THIS IS WHAT'S GREAT ABOUT ROAD TRIPS. EATING IN FUNKY LITTLE DINERS.

I THINK YOU'RE CONFUSING "FUNKY" WITH "DIRTY."
THAT'S WHAT GIVES A PLACE LIKE THIS ATMOSPHERE.

LIGHTEN UP. YOU MIGHT ACTUALLY ENJOY YOURSELF.

MY SPOON JUST WALKED AWAY.
COUNTER'S ROUND. HE'LL BE BACK.

HOW'S EVERYTHING, BOYS?
UMMM, SLIGHT PROBLEM WITH THE TOAST...

I DISTINCTLY ORDERED IT "UMBER" AND THIS IS CLEARLY MORE OF A BURNT SIENNA.

AND HOW ABOUT YOURS, PEE WEE?
MORE HAIR, PLEASE.

HAWTHORNE, I'M NOT SURE ABOUT THIS MOTEL. IT'S NOT LISTED IN MY GUIDE BOOK.
IT'S CHEAP, AND I'M TIRED. LET'S TAKE IT.

WHY SHOULD YOU CARE IF A MOTEL ROOM'S UGLY? YOUR EYES ARE GOING TO BE CLOSED MOST OF THE TIME ANYWAY.

SIGN IN, PLEASE.
OKEY DOKE.

OH, LOOK! THERE MUST'VE BEEN A SMITH FAMILY REUNION HERE.
CASH ONLY.

I LOVE BEING ON THE ROAD. ESPECIALLY WHEN YOU FIRST GET STARTED IN THE MORNING...

A CUP O' JO AND A GLAZED DOUGHNUT, AND YOU'RE OFF TO NEW HORIZONS.

AND THEN THE FAMOUS WILLIE NELSON SONG JUST STARTS PLAYING IN YOUR HEAD.

MOMMAS DON'T LET YOUR BABIES GROW UP TO BE HERMIT CRABS.
ON THE ROAD AGAIN.

THORNTON! THERE YOU ARE!
FILLMORE! HAWTHORNE! WHAT ARE YOU GUYS DOING HERE?

WHEN YOU DIDN'T SHOW UP AT THE LAGOON, HAWTHORNE DECIDED TO COME LOOKING FOR YOU.

HAWTHORNE, YOU OLD SOFTIE. WHAT AN UNSELFISH GESTURE.

HERE'RE MY TRAVEL RECEIPTS. A CHECK WILL BE FINE.
I DIDN'T SIGN OFF ON THIS!

LONG TRAVEL DAY AHEAD OF US. LET'S MAKE THE BEST OF IT.

MAYBE WE COULD PLAY A GAME TO PASS THE TIME?

HOW ABOUT THIS GAME: "TURTLES AND POLAR BEARS KEEP THEIR YAPS SHUT."

I LIKE "CRAB IN THE ARMPIT."
I JUST MADE IT UP.
UMPH!

SO, WHERE ARE WE ANYWAYS? ARE WE GETTING CLOSE TO HOME?
ACCORDING TO THIS MAP WE'RE NEAR THAILAND.
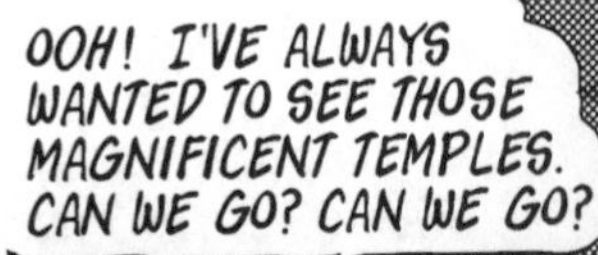

OOH! I'VE ALWAYS WANTED TO SEE THOSE MAGNIFICENT TEMPLES. CAN WE GO? CAN WE GO?

LOOK AT THAT ARCHITECTURE UP AHEAD. IT LOOKS STRANGELY FAMILIAR.
LET'S TAKE A LOOK.

IT'S ODD, BUT I FEEL AT HOME IN THIS TEMPLE.
I KNOW WHAT YOU MEAN.
THIS IS A McDONALD'S!

WELL, BOYS, WE MADE IT. WE'RE BACK IN THE OL' LAGOON.

IT FEELS LIKE HOME ALREADY.

THE SIGHTS... THE SOUNDS...

THE SMELLS.
GUESS HOW MANY WOTTEN CLAMS I HAVE IN MY MOWF.

STAMPEDE! THE HORSES ARE LOOSE!

RUN FOR YOUR LIVES!

WHAT DRAMA COURSE DID HAWTHORNE SIGN UP FOR?
"OVER-ACTING."

SHERMAN'S LAGOON

SHERMAN, WHERE IS THIS PARTY? WE'VE BEEN LOOKING FOR AN HOUR.

THAT MUST BE IT OVER THERE, WHERE ALL THE NOISE IS COMING FROM.

I DON'T THINK THIS IS THE RIGHT PARTY. THERE WOULDN'T BE A MULLET AT OUR PARTY.

THE FISH?
THE HAIRSTYLE.

SAYS HERE THAT SHARK SKIN IS BACK IN FASHION.
THAT'S AN OUTRAGE.

HOW CAN THEY JUSTIFY THE THINGS THEY DO TO INNOCENT ANIMALS?

WELL, IF YOU'RE LUCKY, YOU WON'T GET TURNED INTO A SPORT COAT.
I DON'T NEED LUCK.

I'VE GOT MY TRUSTY RABBIT'S FOOT.
RIGHT.

SHERMAN, TAKE IT OFF!
NO.

MEGAN, MY FRIENDS HAVE COME TO EXPECT ME TO BE THE LIFE OF THE PARTY.

AND I DON'T INTEND TO DISAPPOINT THEM.
DING DONG

HEY! GIANT FOAM FIN. HILARIOUS!
SOME DON'T THINK SO.

Sherman's Lagoon

I THOUGHT YOU WERE GOING TO DO THE LANDSCAPING TODAY.
OH YEAH... RIGHT... THE LANDSCAPING.

WE WERE GOING TO MOVE THAT BOULDER OVER THERE... AND THIS ONE GOES HERE.

AND YOU BOUGHT THESE 3 WEEKS AGO. WE REALLY OUGHT TO PUT THEM IN THE GROUND.

IT'S RAINING.
GET BACK OUT THERE!

WE'LL CATCH THAT SHARK ONE OF THESE DAYS, WATSON.

OH, SURE, HE MIGHT BE MORE CLEVER THAN YOUR AVERAGE SHARK.

BUT SOONER OR LATER I'LL FIND A FLAW IN THAT STEEL TRAP MIND OF HIS, AND THEN HE'LL BE MINE.

DO YOU HAVE TO BUY A VOWEL, OR CAN YOU RENT?
YOU SHOULD STICK WITH CARTOONS.

I'VE HACKED INTO A CORPORATE DATABASE AND I'M PUTTING TERRIBLE THINGS INTO MY SCHOOL COUNSELOR'S CREDIT REPORT.

WHY?
HE TOLD ME TO ABANDON MY CHOSEN CAREER PATH.

WHICH WOULD BE?

EVIL GENIUS.
I'D BE A REFERENCE FOR YOU.

I CAN'T BELIEVE MY EYES! IS IT REALLY TRUE?
OH, HI, MEGAN.

I WAIT AND WAIT FOR THIS ANNUAL EVENT, AND IT'S HERE!

WHY, YES, I'M BACK FROM THE NORTH POLE FOR THE WINTER. I HAD NO IDEA YOU MISSED ME SO MUCH. MEGAN, I'M...

SARDINI'S 24-HOUR SALE!
UH, SURE, YOU CAN BORROW THE PAPER.

SHERMAN'S LAGOON

SHERMAN! SARDINI'S 24-HOUR SALE STARTS IN A COUPLE OF DAYS!

THIS IS GOING TO BE PHYSICALLY EXHAUSTING. WE HAVE TO START DIETING AND EXERCISING RIGHT AWAY!

WHO'S THE OTHER HALF OF "WE"?
MEDICINE BALL. HEADS UP!

MEGAN, WHAT'S WITH THE VIDEO?
IT'S TO HELP WITH THE BIG SALE AT SARDINI'S

IT'S A WORKOUT TAPE THAT TARGETS THE SHOPPING MUSCLES.

MEGAN, THERE'S NO SUCH THING AS A "SHOPPING MUSCLE"!

OKAY, LET'S WORK THOSE RACK-TOIDS.
FEEL MY BIN-CEPS.

HEY, MEGAN, THIS SALE AT SARDINI'S IS SUCH A BIG EVENT, THE LOCAL NEWS IS BROADCASTING IT. WE'RE DOING THE PLAY-BY-PLAY.

AND WHAT A SALE IT SHOULD BE, SHERMAN. THIS FIELD IS FULL OF GRIZZLED VETERANS.

POW!

I MEAN, DELICATE YOUNG FLOWERS.
ROOKIE MISTAKE.

WELCOME BACK TO OUR CONTINUING COVERAGE OF SARDINI'S 24-HOUR SALE.

MEGAN'S HEADING FOR THE HALF-PRICE BIN... BOOM! SHE CLOTHESLINES ANOTHER SHOPPER! WHAT A HIT, FOLKS!

AND THAT'S NOT JUST A FOOTBALL REFERENCE. YOUR WIFE REALLY BELTED HER WITH A CLOTHESLINE!

YOU DIDN'T NEED TO ADD THAT LAST PART.
I'M JUST SAYIN'...
WELL, DON'T.

I KNOW AS BROADCASTERS WE'RE SUPPOSED TO BE IMPARTIAL...

BUT I REALLY HOPE MEGAN WINS THIS SHOPPING CONTEST.

SHERMAN! SHUT UP AND GUARD THESE DELICATES FOR ME!!

CLEAN UP ON AISLE 4. MANHOOD LEAKING EVERYWHERE.
UNGH.

I WON THE SHOPPING CONTEST, SHERMAN. WAS THERE EVER ANY DOUBT THAT I REIGN SUPREME WHEN IT COMES TO SHOPPING?

EVERYTHING WAS 50% OFF.
HOW MUCH DID YOU SPEND?

IT'S NOT HOW MUCH I SPENT, IT'S HOW MUCH I SAVED.
OKAY, HOW MUCH DID YOU SAVE?

AND A PENNY SAVED IS A PENNY EARNED.
ALRIGHTEE, HOW MUCH DID YOU EARN?

SHERMAN'S LAGOON

HI, SHERM.
RUMOR HAS IT YOU HAVE A HAM RADIO ON THE PREMISES.

YEP.

IT'S NOT EDIBLE.
THEN WHY PUT "HAM" IN THE TITLE?!

I'VE PICKED UP SOMEBODY IN THE MIDWESTERN UNITED STATES ON MY HAM RADIO.

SO FAR, I'M JUST GETTING A RHYTHMIC THUMPING. LISTEN.
HMMM.

MAYBE IT'S A DRUMMER IN A FAMOUS ROCK BAND.

HELLO? HELLO? DO YOU READ ME? THIS IS ERNEST. COME IN.
THIS IS RUSTY THE DOG, IN OKLAHOMA.

A DOG? YEAH, RIGHT.

IF YOU'RE A DOG, WHAT'S THREE PLUS FOUR?
THIRTEEN.

IT'S A DOG ALL RIGHT.
I'VE HEARD THEY'RE SMART LIKE THAT.

Sherman's Lagoon

WHAT ARE YOU UP TO ON THIS FINE SUNDAY, HAWTHORNE? ANOTHER DO-IT-YOURSELF HOUSE PROJECT?
YEP.

THE SAME ONE YOU WERE WORKING ON LAST WEEKEND?
NOPE. I'VE GOT A NEW ONE.

REMEMBER HOW I SPENT ALL LAST WEEKEND REPAIRING THE WALL, WHICH WAS DAMAGED WHILE I WAS REPAIRING THE DOOR TWO WEEKENDS AGO?

YEP.
AND THE DOOR WAS MESSED UP BECAUSE I TRIED TO CHANGE THE HINGES THE WEEKEND BEFORE THAT?

UH-HUH.
WHICH WERE BENT WHEN I HAD TO BREAK THROUGH THE DOOR BECAUSE I HAD INSTALLED THE LOCK BACKWARDS THE WEEKEND BEFORE THAT?

UMM, YEP.
WELL, FOR THIS WEEKEND'S DO-IT-YOURSELF PROJECT, I'M GOING TO BLOW UP THE ENTIRE HOUSE AND START OVER!!

MAYBE YOU SHOULD JUST HIRE SOMEBODY TO BLOW UP THE HOUSE.
GIMME A SCREWDRIVER!

YOU'RE TALKING TO A DOG IN OKLAHOMA WITH YOUR HAM RADIO?
YEP. SAY HI, RUSTY.
HERRO.

SO, RUSTY, WHAT'S IT LIKE LIVING WITH HUMANS?
DULL. AFTER WORK, THEY JUST PLOP DOWN ON THE SOFA AND WATCH TV.

WHAT A SAD, PATHETIC LIFE.

DUDE, THAT DESCRIBES YOUR LIFE.
HEY! I DON'T WORK.

ARE YOU TALKING TO THAT DOG VIA HAM RADIO AGAIN?
YEAH. IT'S RUSTY IN OKLAHOMA.

SO, RUSTY, DID YOU HIDE YOUR OWNER'S KEYS, LIKE I TOLD YOU TO?
YEP.

I PUT 'EM IN A PLACE WHERE THEY'LL NEVER LOOK.

COOL. WHERE?
KANSAS.

RUSTY, DO YOUR OWNERS HAVE OTHER PETS?
JUST THE STUPID PARROT I HATE.

MAYBE YOU SHOULD JUST EAT THE THING AND GET IT DONE WITH.

RUSTY? JUST KIDDING. RUSTY?
KLINK KLINK!

WHAT WAS THAT LAST SOUND?
KNIFE IN MAYO JAR, KEMO SABE.

SO, RUSTY, DON'T YOU WISH YOU WERE FREE INSTEAD OF BEING SOMEBODY'S PET?
NAH.

I GET FED WHEN I'M HUNGRY. SOMETIMES THEY RUB MY BELLY. ALL I DO IS LIE ON THE SOFA ALL DAY.

DO YOUR OWNERS NEED A LARGE SHARK?
GIMME THAT!

SO, RUSTY, AS THE FAMILY PET, ARE YOU AN EQUAL WITH THE HUMANS IN THE HOUSE?
NOT EXACTLY.

THEY GET TO POTTY INSIDE, AND I HAVE TO GO OUT IN THE YARD.

BUT THEY GIVE ME A TREAT WHEN I'M DONE...
...TWO IF I GO IN THE NEIGHBOR'S YARD.
SEEMS WORTH THE EFFORT.

SHERMAN, I WANT TO DO SOMETHING SPECIAL FOR OUR ANNIVERSARY.

YOU KNOW WHAT WOULD REALLY MAKE IT UNIQUE?

ME NOT FORGETTING IT?
GOOD START.

Sherman's Lagoon

WELCOME, SHERMAN AND MEGAN TO CHATEAU REQUIN, THE MOST EXCLUSIVE HOTEL IN THE OCEAN.
Front Desk

WE HAVE YOU DOWN FOR ONE NIGHT FOR $400. HOW WILL YOU BE PAYING?

APPARENTLY THROUGH THE NOSE. DIG IN.
SHERMAN!

THIS WILL BE NICE, SHERMAN. A PROFESSIONAL MASSAGE IN AN EXCLUSIVE RESORT.

HOW MUCH ARE THE MASSAGES HERE?
$100 AN HOUR.

YOU'RE AWFULLY TENSE.
ACK!

OOH! I LOVE HOTEL BREAKFAST BARS. COME TO MOMMA.
$40

IS IT ALL YOU CAN EAT?
NOPE. PER PLATE.

$40

AM I STILL CLEAR?
CEILING FAN.

SHERMAN'S LAGOON

MEGAN, YOU'RE NOT ALLOWED TO BRING OUTSIDE SNACKS INTO THESE FANCY HOTELS.

SHERMAN, THIS PLACE IS CHARGING AN ARM AND A LEG FOR EVERYTHING. THIS WON'T HURT THEM.

EXCUSE ME, MA'AM, WHAT'S IN THE SACK?
UH, PRESCRIPTION MEDICINE.

UH, HUH. AND HOW MANY TIMES A DAY DO YOU TAKE YOO-HOO?
THAT'S PERSONAL.

YOU ALL PACKED? IT'S ALMOST CHECK-OUT TIME.
WE'RE ALREADY CHECKED OUT. LOOK. HERE'S OUR "DAILY ROOM CHARGES" SHEET INSIDE OUR USA TODAY.

AUGH! WE MUST'VE ACCIDENTALLY LEFT THE PAY TV CHANNEL ON SINCE WE'VE BEEN HERE!

HOW BAD COULD IT BE?
$250!!

APPARENTLY WE'VE FOUND NEMO 37 TIMES NOW.
YIKES!

YOU DIDN'T EAT THAT GUY. FEELING A LITTLE HUMANITARIAN TODAY?
MAYBE.

DOES IT DEPEND ON WHAT "HUMANITARIAN" MEANS?
MAYBE.

THAT'S THE SECOND DAY YOU'VE PASSED ON A BEACH APE. WHAT'S UP?

SOMETIMES I WONDER IF I'M LOSING MY FEROCIOUS PREDATOR INSTINCT.
I'M SURE IT'S JUST A PHASE.

POOR LITTLE OREO, ALL TWISTED APART.
HEY! IT WAS HIM OR ME!

SHERMAN, I HEARD ABOUT YOU LOSING YOUR FEROCIOUSNESS.
YEP. I'M NOT A MOTIVATED PREDATOR.

WHAT YOU NEED IS A POSTER WITH AN INSPIRATIONAL MESSAGE.
YEAH.

THIS IS A DRINK MENU FROM QUIGLEY'S RESTAURANT.
I USUALLY SALUTE IT.

SHERMAN, THIS IS NED. HE'S GOING TO HELP YOU GET YOUR PREDATOR'S EDGE BACK.

BOY, YOU ARE ONE UGLY DUDE.

YOUR MOMMA TELLS ME YOU WERE SUCH AN UGLY BABY, SHE USED TO PUT THE DIAPER OVER YOUR FACE.

EXCUSE ME. WHAT KIND OF CONSULTANT ARE YOU?
INSULTANT. I'M AN INSULTANT, YOU MORON.

SHERMAN'S LAGOON

ERNEST, I'VE LOST MY MOTIVATION TO BE A PREDATOR.
BUMMER.

I THOUGHT MAYBE YOU COULD FIND SOMETHING ON THE INTERNET TO HELP ME.

LET'S SEE... SOMETHING ON THE INTERNET TO HELP WITH RESTORING MANHOOD...
TAP TAP TAP

NOPE. NOTHING HERE.
GAVE IT A SHOT.

MUST BE TOUGH FOR A SHARK TO LOSE HIS FEROCIOUS PREDATOR NATURE.
SURE IS.

IT'S A STRANGE, CONFUSING TIME FOR ME, ERNEST.

AND I TELL YA... WITHOUT A LOVING, SUPPORTIVE WIFE, I'D BE A WRECK.

HI, ERNEST. HI WIMP.
DEAR.

SHERMAN, I HIRED ANOTHER EXPERT TO HELP YOU WITH YOUR PSYCHOLOGICAL DISORDER.

THIS GUY SAYS HE CAN DO IT. HE'S GOT A PH.D. IN PSYCHOLOGY AND DID HIS THESIS IN MOTIVATION.

DOES HE WEAR THE MIC BECAUSE HE'S USED TO BIG CROWDS?

IT'S FROM HIS DAY JOB.
YOU WANT FRIES WITH YOUR MOTIVATION, SIR?

I HEARD ABOUT YOUR LITTLE PROBLEM. YOU'VE LOST YOUR FEROCIOUS INSTINCT, HUH?
YEAH...

... AND EVERYBODY WANTS TO HELP.

EVERYBODY THINKS THEY'RE A PSYCHOLOGIST.

AS IF MY DEEPLY ROOTED NEUROSIS COULD BE CURED OVER A CUP OF COFFEE.
TELL ME ABOUT YOUR MOTHER. WAS SHE FEROCIOUS?

I'VE COMPLETELY LOST MY MOTIVATION TO BE A FEROCIOUS PREDATOR.
AND, WHY DO YOU THINK THAT IS?

I DON'T KNOW. THAT'S WHY I'M PAYING **YOU**.
AND, WHY DO YOU THINK THAT IS?

BECAUSE YOU SUPPOSEDLY HAVE THE EXPERTISE TO HELP ME WITH MY PROBLEM.
AND, WHY DO YOU THINK THAT IS?

A TAPE RECORDER AND A STUFFED CRAB! AND I'M MAKING $80 AN HOUR RIGHT NOW!
SCHWEET.

I CURED SHERMAN.
THAT'S IMPOSSIBLE. YOU HAVE NO TRAINING IN MEDICINE.

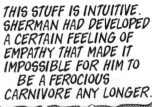

THIS STUFF IS INTUITIVE. SHERMAN HAD DEVELOPED A CERTAIN FEELING OF EMPATHY THAT MADE IT IMPOSSIBLE FOR HIM TO BE A FEROCIOUS CARNIVORE ANY LONGER.

ONCE I DIAGNOSED THE PROBLEM, IT WAS SIMPLY A MATTER OF FINDING THE PART OF HIS BRAIN THAT CONTAINED EMPATHY.

THEN I CUT IT OUT WITH THIS PLASTIC COCKTAIL SWORD.
I HOPE YOU STERILIZED IT.

SHERMAN'S LAGOON

AUGH!

HAWTHORNE! WHAT HAPPENED?
I LOST A CLAW!

SUCK IT UP, CHAMP. YOU'LL GROW A NEW ONE.
BUT, IT'S THE FIRST DAY OF HERMIT CRAB MATING SEASON! THERE'S NO TIME!

CLAWS AREN'T EVERYTHING. WOMEN WANT A CRAB WITH CHARACTER... A CRAB WHO'S FUN.

HOW'S YOUR MATING DANCE?
I'M HORRIBLE AT THE HERMIT CRAB MATING DANCE!

SHOW ME.
YA TA-TA TA-TA TEE TUM TA-TA TA-TA

DOO BOP SHOOBEY DOOBEY DOO BOP

OH MY. ONE CLAW AND SIX LEFT FEET.
I'M DOOMED!

WHAT ON EARTH ARE YOU UP TO?
I'M SETTING UP A PRACTICE.
PSYCHIAT HELP $50/HR.

AFTER THE WAY I HELPED SHERMAN WITH HIS PROBLEM, I FIGURED, WHY NOT?

YOU DIDN'T HELP SHERMAN! YOU PROBABLY MADE HIM WORSE! I HELPED HIM!

WHAT ARE YOU WRITING? IS THAT ABOUT ME?
FILLMORE: ANGER AND PARANOIA ISSUES.

SO, FILLMORE, HOW CAN I HELP YOU?
I NEED TO LEARN TO RELAX.
PSYCHIATRIC HELP $50/HR.

A LITTLE UPTIGHT, HUH?
I ALWAYS FEEL LIKE I HAVE TO BE IN CONTROL... LIKE OTHERS AREN'T DOING THINGS RIGHT.

HMMM.

YOU REALLY SHOULD SIT UP. THAT'S BAD FOR YOUR BACK.
GOLD MINE.

SO, FREDDY, GO ON.
PSYCHIATRIC HELP $50/HR.

WELL, I GUESS AS A FLOUNDER I'VE ALWAYS BEEN SELF-CONSCIOUS ABOUT MY LOOKS.

I GUESS I THOUGHT A LITTLE THERAPY COULD BRING ME SOME SELF-CONFIDENCE.

ARE YOU GOING TO LOOK AT ME?
NOT WITHOUT THE SACK. YOU KNOW THE RULES.

HOW CAN I HELP YOU, SHERMAN?
I HEAR VOICES.

WELL, NOT REALLY VOICES, BUT I DO HEAR A VOICE.
PSYCHIATRIC HELP $50/HR.

WHAT'S THIS VOICE TELL YOU TO DO?
HORRIBLE THINGS.

DO THE DISHES.
THERE. DID YOU HEAR IT?

WHAT'S THE TROUBLE TODAY, FILLMORE?
OH, THE USUAL. JUST LONELY.
PSYCHIATRI HELP

I CRAVE AFFECTION. I WANT TO HOLD SOMEBODY CLOSE. I WANT THEM TO HOLD ME.
HMMM...

LET ME BRING IN MY ASSOCIATE...
OSWALD!
WHO'S HE?

DESIGNATED HUGGER.
AAUUGH!

OKAY, FOLKS, IT'S GROUP THERAPY DAY. LET'S START WITH FILLMORE'S DIFFICULTIES WITH WOMEN.

I'D SAY IT'S HIS AWFUL COLOGNE.

I SAY IT'S HIS POMPOUS, ARROGANT ATTITUDE.

SHOULDN'T HE BE HERE FOR THIS?
WHY? HE'S NOT IN THIS GROUP.

OKAY, IT'S GROUP THERAPY DAY AGAIN. SORRY I'M LATE.

SHERMAN, WHERE'S EVERYONE ELSE?

MMMPHT.

DID YOU EAT THE REST OF THE GROUP?
DON'T SCHEDULE THESE THINGS AT NOON!

WHY ARE YOU CLOSING YOUR PSYCHIATRY PRACTICE, HAWTHORNE?
CLOS

THE BOARD OF PSYCHIATRIC EXAMINERS HAS CONFISCATED MY LICENSE.

THAT'S OKAY. I'LL GO BACK TO SCHOOL AND STUDY TO BE SOMETHING ELSE.

YOUR LAW DEGREE ARRIVED.
PERFECT TIMING.

DOING HOMEWORK?
YEP.

NEED ANY HELP?
SURE. DO YOU REMEMBER HOW TO DO TRIGONOMETRY?

I MEANT "HELP" LIKE SHARPENING YOUR PENCIL OR SOMETHING.
HERE. NOT TOO POINTY.

SHERMAN'S LAGOON

LOOK, GUYS. THE DOCTOR GAVE ME GLASSES. WHADDAYA THINK?

YOU LOOK DIFFERENT.
I FEEL DIFFERENT.

WITH THESE ON, SOMEHOW, I FEEL A LITTLE MORE... FLATULENT.

DID HE MEAN "INTELLIGENT"?
I HOPE SO.

YOU KNOW, MEGAN, SINCE I STARTED WEARING THESE GLASSES, I CAN SEE YOU A LOT MORE CLEARLY NOW.
OLIVE OIL

HMPH.
WHAT IS IT?

I GUESS I ALWAYS THOUGHT YOU WERE... YOU KNOW...

YOU ACTUALLY SAID "PRETTIER"?
WHILE SHE WAS HOLDING A PAN?

IT'S TOUGH BEING US, FILLMORE.
US?

YOU KNOW. THE ONLY SMART ONES IN THE LAGOON.
OH, RIGHT. I FORGOT. YOUR NEW GLASSES HAVE SOMEHOW MADE YOU SMARTER.

SHOULD WE FORM OUR OWN CHAPTER OF MENSA?
NAHH. TOO SEXIST...

... MIGHT UPSET THE WOMENSA.
GOOD POINT.

SHERMAN'S LAGOON

FILLMORE, I FEEL A NEED TO EXPAND MY MUSICAL HORIZONS.
EXCELLENT!

WHO DO YOU WANT TO START WITH? BACH? MOZART? BEETHOVEN? STRAUSS?

WHO WOULD YOU SAY IS THE "WEIRD AL" OF CLASSICAL?
GO.

SHERMAN, THOSE NEW GLASSES OF YOURS DO NOT MAKE YOU INTELLIGENT. THEY JUST MAKE YOU LOOK INTELLIGENT.

TAKE THIS CABBAGE, FOR EXAMPLE... NO GLASSES, JUST ANOTHER DUMB CABBAGE.

GIVE IT GLASSES, AND - PRESTO - IT LOOKS SMART. IT'S ALL APPEARANCES.
HMPH.

GIVE HIM A MULLET AND - PRESTO - HE'S A VEGETABLE AGAIN.
WOW. DO THAT AGAIN.

WHAT? YOU'RE NOT WEARING YOUR EYEGLASSES TODAY?

I DECIDED I DIDN'T NEED THEM.

I HAVE NO USE FOR 20-20 VISION.

MY WORLD IS MORE BEAUTIFUL WHEN IT'S A LITTLE FUZZY.
DO YOU KNOW HIVES WHEN YOU SEE THEM?

SHERMAN'S LAGOON

WHAT DID YOU GIVE MEGAN FOR CHRISTMAS?
TUPPERWARE.
EER

THAT'S NOT VERY CHRISTMASSY.
WE WENT UTILITARIAN THIS YEAR.
BE

IT WAS AN AGREEMENT WE MADE BEFORE THE HOLIDAYS.

EVERY CHRISTMAS WE GIVE EACH OTHER STUFF THAT WE NEVER USE.

TWO YEARS AGO I GOT A TIE I NEVER WEAR.

LAST YEAR I GOT A NOSE HAIR TRIMMER.
BE

SO THIS YEAR WE AGREED OUR GIFTS SHOULD BE SOMETHING THAT WE NEED IN A BIG WAY.

WHAT DID SHE GIVE YOU?
A NOSE HAIR TRIMMER.
BE